Essentials of Trading:

It's Not WHAT You Think
It's HOW You Think

Larry Pesavento
with
Leslie Jouflas

Traders Press, Inc.®
PO Box 6206
Greenville, SC 29606

http://www.traderspress.com

ISBN: 0-934380-93-7
Published by Traders Press, Inc.®

Editing by:
Teresa Darty Alligood
Layout and Cover Design by: Teresa Alligood
Traders Press, Inc.®

Traders Press, Inc.®
PO Box 6206
Greenville, SC 29606

Books and Gifts
for Investors and Traders

Trading Essentials Article Titles:

"Many times the reading of a book
has made the fortune of a man—
has decided his way in life.

"To use books rightly is to go to them for help:
to appeal to them when our knowledge and power fail;
to be led by them into wider sight and clear
conception of our own."

—Ralph Waldo Emerson

"You have to be willing to make mistakes regularly; there is nothing wrong with it...making your best judgment, being wrong, making your next best judgment, being wrong, making your third best judgment, and then doubling your money."
Bruce Kovner—"Market Wizards,"
by Jack Schwager

A Tribute to John Hill

It was in the early "70's" that I first met John Hill. The markets had decimated my account as I proceeded to break every investment law ever written. As a 30-year old, the bounce-back is usually quick but it is a painful process. John Hill became my mentor and led me toward the old masters of trading to understand how the markets operated. Livermore, Gartley, Wycoff, Gann, Cole, Dunnigan, Shabacker, Bayer and many of the other old masters were studied. Over the next few years, with John's guidance, I amassed an extensive library. This library grew quite large over the next 30 years.

Several years ago, John Hill formed *Futures Truth* to promote fairness and honesty in advertising in the futures markets. *Futures Truth* Magazine has come under attack from unscrupulous vendors but *Futures Truth* always prevailed.

To this day, meeting John Hill was one of the most fortunate days of my life. The real tribute to a man's life on earth is the legacy he leaves. And Mr. Hill has a jeweled one! All three of his children, John Jr., Holliston, and Lundy have made very successful careers in trading. *"A teacher affects eternity; he can never tell where his influence stops"* – Henry Adams. John and his wife Carol still live and trade in their farm in the North Carolina Mountains. I had the good fortune to visit them several times. John is now 74 but he still looks and acts exactly as I knew him over 30 years ago. He trades every day.

Here are some of the attributes of John Hill – my trading mentor:

1. Experience – a seasoned veteran who has seen both bull and bear markets and thrived.

2. Knowledge – an avid searcher of the cause and effect of the markets to find what would work and what would not.

3. Patience – waiting for the right time to explain or illustrate an idea or concept.

4. Fortitude – staying with you as your friend and mentor when you think you cannot come back from the abyss.

5. Honesty – teaching that honesty with yourself is most important, and promoting this honesty with everyone who would come in contact with him.

Those of us that have been blessed with John Hill as our friend will cherish it forever. He has changed countless lives through his unconditional sharing. We all love you – good buddy!

2 teach
\+ is
2 change lives
――――――
4 ever

"I always say that you could publish trading rules in the newspaper and no one would follow them. The key is consistency and discipline. Almost anybody can make up a list of rules that are 80 percent as good as what we taught our people. What they couldn't do is give them the confidence to stick to those rules even when things are going bad."

Richard Dennis—"Market Wizards,"
by Jack Schwager

A Wish versus a Decision

There is a huge difference between a wish and a decision. A wish is negative and puts the trader in a frozen state waiting for something to happen (usually related to bailing them out of a losing position). This is negatively charged energy. Decisions on the other hand are positively charged energy. It makes the trader take action. Taking action is taking responsibility! You alone are responsible for your current mental state or condition. Decisions can be both good and bad. The sooner the trader realizes the bad decision, the sooner he can act to correct it.

The first step in the decision making process is to realize that what you are doing is not working. Remember that falling down is a positive motion if you bounce right back! Make a list of the positive and negative things that will happen when you take action on the decision.

Don't expect instant gratification if you make the decision. Decision-making is a process that begins with the first step but these steps are the foundation for a stronger behavioral structure. A stronger behavioral structure will give the trader confidence in his or her trading. Confidence plays a key role in successful trading. Having the confidence necessary for successful trading can help the trader in difficult trading environments. Whereas one trader lacking the confidence and good decision making skills may be frozen and unable to act, the trader who has taken the time to build this foundation will be prepared to take the appropriate actions.

Many times specific decisions a trader makes will not yield profits, they will result in a loss, but more importantly it will position the trader to be able to recognize and act on the next opportunity. Practicing and applying this process will pay dividends throughout your lifetime!

"It was at that point that I said, "Mr. Stupid, why risk everything on one trade? Why not make your life a pursuit of happiness rather than pain?" That was when I first decided I had to learn discipline and money management. It was a cathartic experience for me, in the sense that I went to the edge, questioned my very ability as a trader, and decided that I was not going to quit. I was determined to come back and fight. I decided that I was going to become very disciplined and businesslike about my trading."

Paul Tudor Jones—
"Market Wizards," by Jack Schwager

A Radio Interview with Larry Pesavento

1. How did you first become interested in trading?

I began in 1959 when I was a freshman in college, my uncle had given me a stock tip called elastic stop nut. I told a few of my fraternity brothers who in turn told their fathers, it turned out to be a good tip so I supplied them with the stocks my Uncle was buying not knowing it was a huge bull market in everything and I craved the attention.

2. When first starting in this business what do you feel was your worst trading error?

This is by far the toughest question because I have made so many errors. It has been said that the smart man learns from his mistakes, but the wise man learns from the mistakes of others, I was not a wise man because I had made many mistakes many times, usually the same ones. But by far the worst thing that you can do in trading is to add to a losing position. It is followed closely by trading without a trading plan or money management.

3. At what point did you realize that trading was a career and a business that was for you and why?

It was the 1967 silver market and I did very well in that but the real key was that trading was the last thing I thought about before going to sleep. I dreamt it all night and it was the first thing I thought about in the morning.

4. Psychologically how do you treat losses and account draw downs?

Losses in trading are like breathing, you can't live in this business without breathing. Mark Douglas taught me to think in probabilities and to not rely on any particular trade. If your methodology is correct, a string of losers will be followed by winning streaks.

5. Looking back who are the people you respected and modeled in the trading profession?

John Hill, Amos Hostetter, Bryce Gilmore and Mark Douglas.

6. As one of the foremost Fibonacci experts in the trading world, would you consider this your number one technical tool for market entry and exit?

The use of Fibonacci numbers is probably one of the most misunderstood concepts in technical analysis. It is a part of an area of study called Sacred Geometry. Within this structure are the non-random patterns in the stock market that repeat daily and can be quantified and traded profitably. Without this I would have no way of measuring risk and therefore no trading plan.

7. WITH THE HUNDREDS OF TECHNICAL INDICATORS OUT THERE WHAT WOULD YOU SUGGEST NEW TECHNICIANS DO TO PREVENT "ANALYSIS PARALYSIS"?

Find a strategy that they like and understand and implement it with good money
management strategy. This question has implications that most traders are always searching for the Holy Grail; the Holy Grail is that nine inch cycle that extends from your left ear over the top of your head to your right ear. Once the trader recognizes that he has no control over which trades are profitable or how much he can make on any one trade with any certainty he will come to realize that the only thing that the trader can control is the risk on any one trade.

8. WHEN DID YOU FIRST ACTUALLY TRADE THE MARKETS?

In my past lives I traded Egyptian palm oil with the Pharaohs in Egypt while studying the Fibonacci numbers of the pyramid at Giza. I surfaced again in 1965 when I started trading cattle and silver actively along with some stocks. I only traded from the long side I did not know how to put on a short sale.

9. DO YOU REMEMBER YOUR FIRST MAJOR TRADE AND THE THINKING BEHIND IT?

This should be a two-part question, was it the first major trade before I knew something, or when I knew nothing? The first major trade when I knew nothing was a Wheat spread and I took off the short side of the spread and remained long. It just happened to be the day before the Great Russian grain robbery was announced. After I lost everything and I began to study the markets the trade that got me back to where I was happened to be the big soybean market of 1976-1977.

10. What is your most memorable trade?

There have been so many that I think about often but one that is similar to the current news was the January 1991 trade that contained three parts. I am a pattern recognition trader, I try to take every identifiable pattern within my equity limits. In January of 1991, two days before the desert storm war on Iraq, I had a major sell signal in gold and crude oil and a huge bullish Gartley pattern in the SP 500. It was the day of the solar eclipse and new moon of January when the bombs hit Baghdad at midnight Baghdad time. The markets were closed in the U.S. and there was no overnight S&P trading. Several friends called me to tell me what was happening and I watched what was happening with a bomb by bomb description of what was happening in Baghdad. Early unconfirmed reports by the financial press alluded to soaring gold and crude oil prices accompanied by plunging stock prices. In the next few hours however, it was apparent that this was going to be one of the shortest wars in history and the allies had brought Iraq to their knees. The next day opened down the $25 oz permissible limit, crude oil fell over $10 barrel ($10,000 per contract) making it the largest percentage drop in crude oil in history. On the next day following the war, the stock market experienced one of its largest percentage gains in its 200-year history.

11. What advice would you give someone in regards to being successful in the markets?

First remember trading is a journey not a destination and read every thing available that concerns the psychology of the market place and you. Find a mentor that has successfully beaten the markets and emulate his or her strategy, but be sure that it conforms to your belief structure and risk perimeters.

12. What mistakes do most people make in the markets?

No money management and no trading plan and not trading the plan if they have one. Losers think how much can I win - Winners think how much can I lose. The reason this is so important is because risk is the only thing a trader can control. Losers habitually focus on how much profit they are going to make winners correctly focus on executing the trading plan and thinking in probabilities.

13. How did you end up becoming a trader?

One of my favorite hobbies is to read Chinese literature and a particular quote by Confucius has always stuck with me – *The man who loves his job is always on vacation*. It's the greatest profession in the world because you have total freedom; you are your own boss. It's different every day and you meet some of the nicest people in the world and your success can be limitless.

14. What do you think are the greatest misconceptions people have about the markets?

First, markets are chaotic in nature, but within this chaos are non-random patterns that repeat and are predictable. Second, trading is simple but it's not easy. The process of making it easy can take years, but the main thing to remember is to never give up. Third, the news follows the trends. Enron was going down a whole year before it filed bankruptcy as well as Kmart and Lucent and others. But by far the greatest misconception about the market is the lack of respect given to the science of the planetary cycles of the market. Those of us (and we are very few) have done considerable research and very little of it is recognized. At this stage of my life it really means less to me than it did earlier because I was able to profit from it. I've proven to myself beyond any reasonable doubt that there is a strong correlation between these cycles and movements in the stock market and commodity markets as well. A case in point is the Bradley stock market cycle that does an amazing job of forecasting turning points in the market year after year.

"The elements of good trading are: (1) cutting losses, (2) cutting losses, and (3) cutting losses. If you can follow these three rules, you may have a chance.

Ed Seykota—"Market Wizards," by Jack Schwager

Anger In Trading

Trading while in a state of anger is a surefire recipe for disaster. Trading in anger takes two forms. First - anger against the market which traditionally leads to revenge trading by trying to recoup your losses because the market failed to meet your expectations! Markets are seldom wrong – men often are. If this type of anger is a frequent occurrence then you should seek professional help immediately. That type of anger is deeply seeded in the trader's psyche and goes beyond the scope of this trader's experience.

Anger coming from outside the market environment is more frequent and more easily identified and correctable. The source of this anger is usually related to personal relationships or outside business events. This can be as trivial as normal bill paying or car problems or parental responsibilities. Sometimes these are minor distractions and not anger triggered.

Anger takes energy away from the responsibility of strict risk management. The trader must learn to acknowledge the presence of an outside distraction. Traders who use well thought out trade plans are less susceptible to distractions. Those without trade plans are at the mercy of the market. Some words of advice – if the anger is bothering you at any level take a break until the culprit is out of your system. It will prove to be the best trading decision of the day!

"I don't think traders can follow rules for very long unless they reflect their own trading style. Eventually, a breaking point is reached and the trader had to quit or change, or find a new set of rules he can follow. This seems to be part of the process of evolution and growth of a trader."

Ed Seykota—

"Market Wizards," by Jack Schwager

Ask for the Best and Expect to Get it

One of my favorite hobbies is collecting books. These are my most treasured friends. Common threads run through these writings, from the ancient to the latest. The Holy Bible, writings of Confucius, Koran, Hebrew Bible, sayings of Buddha, etc.

The following tenets to success are from Terry Cole Whittaker a very popular minister in the Southern California area. They are simple to understand and easy to implement. If only one of my readers can use these then this article was very rewarding to the both of us! The additional comments under each tenet are my own.

1. Desire the top most - "The ancestry of every action is thought" – Emerson
2. Pray and ask for what you desire - "Ask and you shall receive" The Bible
3. Seek knowledge of how to attain the ultimate - Read books go to lectures, ask questions, and find a mentor. There is a plethora of great source material available and most of it is very affordable.

4. Do what works and don't do what doesn't - Be comfortable with learning! Make it Fun! Life can be a real journey to a fabulous destination.
5. Control your mind and be positive - If you would like to win but think you can't it is almost a cinch you won't. Life's battles don't always go to the stronger or faster man. But sooner or later the one who wins is the one who thinks he can.
6. Upgrade on a regular basis - Life is a journey – not a destination! Surround yourself with positive friends and if they are not then make it a project to change them. Read and listen to inspirational material as part of your daily ritual. Regarding trading; read 4 to 5 pages of Mark Douglas' book 'Trading in the Zone" which will enrich your trading immensely.
7. Keep on keeping on! - There is no disgrace in failing. The disgrace comes when you don't continue. At the depths of England's entry into WWII, Sir Winston Churchill addressed a prominent college here is his entire speech; "Don't ever give up – Never, Never, Never!"

"The most important thing is money management, money management, money management. Anybody who is successful will tell you the same thing. The one area that I am constantly trying to improve on is to let my gains run. I'm not able to do that well. I'm always working on it. To my dying day, I'll probably still be working on it."
Marty Schwartz—
"Market Wizards," by Jack Schwager

Barking Up the Wrong Tree

Many traders who have gone through the boom/bust cycle start looking for a "new" method of trading to relieve them of this painful cycle.

During this search the trader incorrectly directs his or her focus of attention to how much money someone else makes with this new system. They ask irrelevant questions such as, "What percentage are you up?" and "How much did you make last year?" Instead, the trader should learn to evaluate a system based on it's own merits, i.e., is the method capable of making money over the long term, does the method trade low risk/high probability setups, can the risk be quantified, is the risk acceptable, are there built in profit taking objectives and can I employ a good money management system?

I always wonder what the person is really seeking in these questions. Security, comfort or even a guarantee they will make money?

Trading is an independent and many times a solitary endeavor. It requires that the trader be focused on the process, not the outcome.

When a trader asks these types of questions it shows they are seeking comfort and are focused on the outcome and not on the process.

Another irrelevant question frequently asked is "Which way do you think the market is headed"? "I don't know", is my usual reply. The person is usually surprised because they have a pre-conceived idea that traders should know which way the market is going. They do not yet understand trading in terms of probabilities.

The results of one method executed by multiple traders can have a very wide range of results based on many things including the skill level and experience of the individual trader and most importantly how well each individual trader can follow the rules of the method. A trader with 2 years experience will not be at the same skill level of a trader with 10 years experience.

Whatever methodologies of trading you choose to study do yourself a great service and shift your focus to the process. If you try and skip parts of the process you will only harm yourself by not gaining and learning the subtle and necessary pieces of information to be successful.

Be willing to commit to whatever time line it takes you as an individual to be a successful trader.

"The best traders can put on a trade without the slightest bit of hesitation or conflict, and just as freely and without hesitation or conflict, and admit it isn't working. They can get out of the trade—even with a loss—and doing so doesn't resonate the slightest bit of emotional discomfort."
Mark Douglas—"Trading in the Zone"

Be Smart – Not Stubborn

The legendary trader Paul Tudor Jones states that "It's much better to lose your opinion instead of your money." This is a profound statement from a true market sage. How many of us have held positions day after day as our equity eroded only to have to exit the position later and usually near the end of the move.

Be ever mindful that your trading capital is your financial seed. You must not let the pigeons and crows get at it before you have a chance to plant them and see them grow. There are two things I always do to keep the birds from my seeds;

First - The three day rule; pattern recognition is a leading indicator of future price action not lagging as are all moving average and oscillator systems. These patterns have a mathematical probability assigned to them and they usually work immediately. The 3 day rule is simple – If your position is not profitable at the end of the third trading day, exit the position on the close of the third day. This rule has saved my bacon many times and never made me regret exiting the trade.

Second - Order entry – Order exit! For many years I have used the same broker. He will not take an order from me without placing a corresponding stop loss at the same time! This rule protects the trader from his greatest enemy – himself! Desk stops (those on your desk and not placed in the market) are never filled! A great deal of comfort is obtained by having your stop in the market. It's such a simple thing to implement and make a habit!

Try these two rules for yourself. They save a lot and cost so little!

"Traders who are consistently successful are consistent as a natural expression of who they are. They don't have to try to be consistent: they are consistent. This may seem like an abstract distinction, but it is vitally important that you understand the difference. Being consistent is not something you can try to be, because the very act of trying will negate your intent by mentally taking you out of the opportunity flow, making it less likely that you will win and more likely you will lose."
Mark Douglas—"Trading in the Zone"

Build Your Trading House

The foundation of a good trading strategy is discipline. Discipline must extend to all areas of your life. Meditation, exercise, positive thinking, sound work ethics are areas essential when discipline is concerned!

The trading house is composed of walls, windows and doors in addition to the foundation! The walls consist of your trading methodology. This develops over time and shows the importance of the foundation. Without a sound foundation, the trading methodology will be different to complete and maintain.

Windows and doors are my favorite parts of the house. There can be many, many windows and doors. This is your money management and risk control segment of your trading house. Think of the windows and doors as the exits where your equity leaves the trading house. One of my favorite quotes from the movies was referring to this process. As Mr. Bond enters the room he says, "I never enter a room unless I can see every way there is to get out of it." What great trading advice! Before entering trades take a look and incorporate in your plan every type of outcome you can think of and be prepared for it. As an example, using time stops, will this be a potential reverse trade if price does this, etc. Focus on the amount of money at risk in your trading house! Keep the doors and windows under surveillance at all times. Be quick to close them if the equity starts to escape.

The last part of the house is the roof. It is the covering that protects the rest of the house. Consider it the nails holding the structure together. It is the commitment to do the business of trading successfully no matter how long it takes! Rome was not built in a day!

"For your mind to be open to a true exchange of energy, you can't be in a state of knowing or believing that you already know what's going to happen next. When you are at peace with not knowing what's going to happen next, you can interact with the market from a perspective where you will be making yourself available to let the market tell you, from its perspective, what is likely to happen next. At that point, you will be in the best state of mind to spontaneously enter "the zone," where you are tapped into the "now moment opportunity flow."

Mark Douglas—"Trading in the Zone"

Chance Favors the Prepared Mind

These words of Thomas A. Edison are important in any endeavor but particularly true in the trading arena. Trading is not just about trade preparation it is also about mental preparation. Mental preparation should occur first and foremost. Traders must learn to think in probabilities. Recognition of the mental preparation in trading is the first step in the success pattern of the good trader. No one knows what will happen next nor do we know which trades will work. All the trader can do is control the risk. Prepare your mind to think in terms of how much capital is at risk on any one trade, and not in terms of how much you can win.

Have a plan to prepare yourself mentally, physically and emotionally for trading each day. It's not *what* you think in trading – it's *how* you think!

"The success in trading comes not from knowing a myriad of patterns or technicals, etc., but from the way you organize your day and the consistency of your approach."
Linda Bradford Raschke

CHANGE YOUR SHOES

There is an old Chinese adage that states until you have walked in another man's shoes be not hard to judge. And one of the most popular lines from a religious poem is; "I was sad because I had no shoes until I met the man who had no feet." There is always going to be people with less than you and more than you. Only one person is at the top and only one person is at the bottom. The top person is the one who is truly thankful and happy at where they are at that moment. The bottom person lives in misery and despair with no hope for improvement. These conditions have very little to do with money or possessions. It is the state of mind that determines your happiness. Lottery winners have been studied years after they won the huge prize. The results were amazing. Many had spent it all and were back where they started. There were divorces and suicides as well as horrible stories of illness (both physical and mental). Money can not buy health and peace of mind.

Our glass of life is either half full or half empty. It is our choice at how we like to see the glass. Things are never as good as they appear or as black as they appear to be. Start learning how to focus on the positive. One of my personal favorites was the work of Tony Robbins. He uses Neural Linguistic Programming (NLP) to change beliefs and attitude. Some of his success stories are truly amazing. He markets a set of CD's and tapes called 'Personal Power" that are well worth their several hundred dollar cost. If you can't spend that amount get a book by James Allen, 'As a Man Thinketh'. Written over 60 years ago, the book relates how our minds control our circumstances.

Try to do something positive each day. Whether or not you believe, it you really are the "Captain of your ship and the Master of your soul."

If you think you are beaten, you are. If you think you dare not, you won't. If you would like to win but think you can't, it's almost a cinch you won't. Life battles don't always go to the stronger or faster man; but the one who wins is the man who thinks he can!

"Goals are something that can be continuously updated and should be reviewed every day. KNOW YOUR GOALS. Have a PLAN... You will always have your best odds of success in achieving your outcome if you have a written down PLAN."
Linda Bradford Raschke

Change Your Thoughts

If a man is to change his world it is first necessary to change his thoughts. Change a thought and you can change a habit. Changing a habit is like weaving a steel cable day after day until it becomes unbreakable.

Denial is one emotion that interferes with our ability to change our behavior. Denial is one of our psychological mechanisms that help us to overcome fear. Fear is the greatest obstacle to the success of a trader. It shatters the very foundation of consistency and confidence in trading. Fear can be broken down through this acronym:

F.E.A.R. = **F**alse **E**vidence **A**ppearing **R**eal.

This false evidence appears in many forms to the trader such as fear of failure, financial ruin, loss of freedom, etc. The list of fears can go on indefinitely. Almost all fears never materialize. This leaves only one alternative if you want to be a successful trader. Face your fears one at a time and break them down into their most basic components.

For example, you have a fear of losing money. Well no one likes to lose money do they? If we are willing to accept that we can lose money then we should be able to accept that this has an associated risk. Ask yourself what is the worst possible thing that could go wrong with the trade and what would be the best possible outcome that could happen with the trade? Somewhere in between these two extremes is the logical outcome.

Through this process of facing your fears you arrive at the true essence of trading – control of risk! It is the only factor you can control when trading. We never know how much we are going to make on a trade or even if we are going to be right on a trade! Only the amount of capital at risk is within our control. Once this realization hits you as a trader the process of trade execution and trade management is greatly simplified. Remember one very important fact – Trading is simple but it isn't easy!

"... It takes time for your routine and good habits to become automatic and natural. It can take weeks and months to see the eventual payoff. But, in the long run, commitment and patience will pay off. Those who are persistent WILL see the payoff. There are few things more satisfying than becoming proficient in your chosen field or discipline, and knowing that the rewards of hard work and intensive study are there to be reaped. Whatever picture you put in your mind, you will be able to achieve!"

Linda Bradford Raschke

Charting your Equity

An overlooked technique by most traders is that of charting their equity changes. Most traders just look at daily net changes; few go to the trouble of charting the equity each day. You will be surprised to learn that it will look like any other stock or commodity chart. Each trader is susceptible to mood (and equity) swings. During my years at Commodity Corporation this was done for you by the firms' computers and was waiting on your desk each morning. These equity charts were reviewed by the peer committee and was heavily weighted as to the amount of equity you were given to trade. The peer review was alert to abnormal swings, both positive and negative.

Charting you equity each day will be a wealth of information to you. You will notice trends in your trading that can be further analyzed by using a diary. It will graphically depict danger signs in equity swings. Sometimes the dollar amount is not as important as percent of equity fluctuations. The daily equity graph will illustrate how you are handling risk!

The great traders will not show large fluctuations in their daily equity graphs. Commodity Corporation was blessed to have Amos Barr Hostetter as one of its directors and traders. Amos was the standard that everyone strived to emulate. One of my closest friends and trading buddies was Jay Krosp who worked side by side with Amos during the early years at Commodity Corporation. Jay was given the task of analyzing the trades made by Amos. Every year was a winning year and rates of return ranged from 35% a year on the lower end to hundreds of percent on the high end. Amos knew how to let his profits run. He used to *say "Take care of your losses, and the profits will take care of themselves."*

He hand posted his bar charts and equity each day and urged all of his disciples (many became Market Wizards) to do the same!

"If you cannot lose cheerfully, do not trade in the market! It is no business for the person who is easily discouraged. Countless losses must be accepted: The problem is to limit the losses. No one may ever hope to become so expert that he never takes a loss."

Humphrey B. Neill—
"Tape Reading and Market Tactics," 1931

Cherry Picking

The opposite of learning to think in probabilities is to try and "Cherry Pick" your trades. Cherry picking refers to the process of trying to isolate only the very best trades. The problem with this concept is that there are no very best trades. They are all the best trades. The problem is we don't know which ones will work. The two things that are certain in trading is that we will never know which trade is going to win and we will never know how much we will make on any trade. The only controllable is how much we have at risk on any particular trade.

Losers are results oriented and winners are execution oriented. Losers think how much can I make – winners think how much can I lose. Cherry picking is like being on death row, it's only a matter of time before your number is called. You must learn to treat all patterns the same – as a probability not a certainty. Cherry pickers are defensive traders! Experience has taught me one great lesson and that is the very best trades I find are seldom the very best trade. The reason for this is if a perfectly symmetrical pattern fails it will offer another opportunity in the opposite direction. When the patterns fail they tend to move a long way in the opposite direction.

Trading is an unknown entity. Risk is all we ever know. Focus your attention on the risk. Take care of your losses and the profits take care of themselves!

"Another observation on mistakes is that the trader who is right in his analysis 60% of the time and makes mistakes in less than 10% of his trades will make money. The trader who is right in his analysis 80% of the time and makes mistakes 20% of the time will lose."

Roy W. Longstreet—
"Viewpoints of a Commodity Trader"

Confidence in Trading

Confidence comes in many forms related to trading. There is over-confidence and under-confidence, both of which can lead to very serious trading problems. Over-confidence occurs when the trader has had a string of winners and feels indestructible. A common statement made is something like, "I thought I knew more than the markets" or "I thought I had trading figured out." The trader will usually begin to get sloppy in their trading and take poor risk/reward trades. Hard earned profits can disappear in a very short time if over-confidence is present unless the trader has learned techniques to recognize this and nip it in the bud.

Under-confidence occurs when the trader either can't pull the trigger or has trouble staying in a trade because he lacks confidence of his analysis and price objectives. These errors result in lost opportunities and money left on the table.

Many times when trading errors are present as a pattern, the trader assumes if they can just have confidence it will solve many trading problems. But if too much is harmful and too little is harmful then what is the correct type of confidence to have in trading? I believe many traders believe that if they just have a string of winners that will give them the confidence they need to forge ahead. Yes, sometimes a winner can give you some confidence to get in the next trade, but what about the other side of the coin? The side of the coin that is on the losing side? Can there be confidence on the losing side of trading?

After many ups and downs with "confidence" I finally learned that my true confidence comes not with my winning trades but in my ability to control the losers and manage my trades. I noticed a consistent positive attitude that was associated and linked with how I was handling my losses! I started to feel *good* about how I would take a loss. There was an immediate down emotional feeling if I experienced a larger loss than necessary or exceeded a maximum daily loss. So that led me to change the behavior that led to that feeling that *I didn't like*. AHA! I had control of that. I can not control the markets, but I can sure control my trades, i.e., entries, exits, stops, how much I trade during the day, how many positions at one time, etc.! (With the rare exception of course, of unexpected market events).

I was asked recently by a newer trader how I build my confidence. I told them that my confidence comes from my controlling the losers, not from the winners, to strive for excellence in learning to manage your trades and feel *good* about the losers!

"Rule 20 Concentrate on how you are playing, not on whether you are winning.

"The idea of winning money, as we have seen, is a false goal. You can actually be playing quite poorly and be winning quite handily. This is not the victory it feels like, however, for eventually this bad play will catch up to disastrous if you are achieving this by playing wrong. (Probably the thing we should hope for is to lose when we are playing wrong, for this will steer us toward the correct path.)"

Larry W. Phillips—"The Tao of Poker"

CYCLES AND OBJECTIVITY

Nature has many cycles that are not controlled by mankind. But mans responses to these events can vary widely in degree and that intensity of degree is determined by how close it is to any particular individual or individuals. People will attach a negative or positive perspective of the event. The responses will vary in degree depending on how close of a connection a person has to the event.

For example, if an avalanche of huge proportions in the remote, uninhabited mountains of Alaska occurs, no towns destroyed or people killed or injured, then it is viewed as a natural event without much, if any, emotion attached to it and it is not likely a positive or negative perspective will be attached to the event.

If an avalanche of the same proportions occurred at the top of a town and destroyed the town in it's path the response would be quite different and many emotions would be attached to the event. The perception of the event would change. It would no longer be a normal cycle of nature but now a tragedy and catastrophe.

The fact of the matter would still remain that the act of nature is simply what it is. The act itself carries no opinion or intent. It is a cycle that must complete so that a new cycle can begin.

If a trader can view price movement as a cycle and that it is simply what it is and the opportunity for profit will be at it's greatest at point "X" of the cycle then it is quite possible to change their mindset from one of opinion to one of objectivity. The mindset that is the closest to objective will be able to view the price movement and cycles for what they are, nothing more and nothing less.

There are many cycles of varying degrees and strengths around us everyday and we simply take those in stride. Some are; the Sun rising in the east and setting in the west. The Moon rising, the temperature during the day rising and falling. Perhaps it rained or was a pleasant sunny day. The wind during the fall is part of a cycle. If you have a cat that sleeps 18 hours a day, that is part of a cycle also. You're eating habits, moods, work times, recreation times, the markets opening and closing, etc.

When you find yourself attaching emotion to your trades remember that the price is in a cycle of it's own, a part of nature. It is simply what it is. Learn to recognize signs of the beginning, middle and ends of the markets cycles.

"The Vision that you glorify in your mind, the Ideal that you enthrone in your heart—this you will build your life by, this you will become."
James Allen— "As A Man Thinketh"

DEALING WITH THE UNEXPECTED

Sooner or later in your trading career something unexpected will happen that will have the potential to do some damage to your account. It could come in the form of an unexpected change in interest rates, a statement made by a political or economic leader. It could be from a news announcement made by a large market moving company or from world events. It could be from something like a power outage in your area that is not affecting the markets, just you! Or it could come from an electronic meltdown at one of the exchanges. Whatever or wherever the source it is best to have a plan of action when these things occur.

If you are so lucky that it is working in your favor consider taking the windfall by closing the position and counting your lucky stars. If a sudden move happens quickly many times it will reverse just as quickly.

You could consider having a backup for your computer, many laptops now can be equipped with wireless internet connections at reasonable monthly rates, and in the case of a power outage this could save you a lot of money by being able to access your account online. Many times power outages will also affect telephone lines so having your cell phone charged up at all times is a great way to be prepared (same with having your laptop batteries charged). It would be unfortunate to have failed to keep your laptop or cell phone charged up in the event of a power failure.

I have a personal policy to close any positions that are open when something unexpected such as a power outage occurs or my data sources go dead.

When an adverse move happens and catches you on the wrong side of the market you must know in advance how you will handle that. A couple of options are; closing the position immediately, or in the event of a gap opening wait for the first 15 -20 minutes of trading, if there is no reversal of price then you must exit and take the loss. In the case of S&P 500 trading you could hedge your position or trade the SPY in place of it if trading happened to shut down for one reason or another in that market.

Money management becomes critical when faced with adverse situations in trading. To start with **never** go into the initiation of any trade with a position larger than you should be trading to start with! The trading gods frown on this and they will let you know! If you have done it before and it worked you are on borrowed time.

If you end up with a larger than expected loss, brush yourself off and look for the next opportunity because the unexpected will *always* happen.

Take some time to plan out your personal first aid trading plan.

"He who has conquered failure. His every thought is allied with power, and all difficulties are bravely met and wisely overcome. His purposes are seasonably planted, and they bloom and bring forth fruit which does not fall prematurely to the ground. Thought allied to purpose becomes creative force..."

James Allen— "As A Man Thinketh"

Deep Silence Brings Deep Listening

Within the deep recesses of our mind and soul are incredible mechanisms that allow us to answer many of life's important questions. Problems arise because our minds have so much clutter thrown at them at any given time. Have any of us ever experienced real silence? Deep sleep qualifies but our dreams control what happens during sleep. Recently the introduction of sensory deprivation tanks has approached the subject on a scientific basis. Frankly it is my opinion that laying in a salt-water solution in a totally dark soundproof environment is not my idea of fun.

Deep silence leads to deep listening! As a trader it is so very important to think about the whole process of trading. Silence and listening are two of the trader's most important tools.

Mark Douglas uses the tapes from the Monroe Institute in North Carolina. Others use natural sounds of nature and the works of the great composer's, Mozart, Beethoven, Wagner and others.

With silence and listening will come control of your thoughts.

These are your thoughts and are coming from inside your mind. Keep your own counsel by not listening to others. Silence and listening will help you focus on your goals. They will help you to listen to what the market is saying. Remember the old trading adage *"Markets are seldom wrong – but men often are."*

Keep the silence and listening on a positive format. Focus on what is right in your life. The glass should always be half full – never half empty. Nothing will destroy your trading (and your life) faster or more effectively than focusing on the negative aspects of anything. What you think about is what you become.

Think about what you want to be during your times of deep silence and deep listening. It just might transform your entire outlook on trading and life. Bookstores and libraries are filled with self-help books on the subject.

"Trade what the market IS—
Not what the market IS NOT—
Traders that trade the market that IS—
Are truly the happiest lot."
Gary Porter

Despair

When all hope is nearly gone or seems that it is gone, it is most probably the exact point for a change of events. The tide is always highest at its peak! The Bible refers to despair as the most dangerous of sins. During my three-year stint at Commodity Corporation, our trading peers had developed a program to deal with despair. First, they recognized the three major causes of despair, death, divorce and a debilitating loss in capital. Any one of these events puts the trader on a one-month (with pay) trading sabbatical. After the one month sabbatical, the peer committee would meet each day to review trade status and evaluate the mental and physical state of the trader. A board-certified psychiatrist was on retainer at Commodity Corporation for this specific purpose.

It was very rare for a seasoned trader to be under peer review for very long. However, newer traders were the target of the peer group scrutiny.

Most of us do have a psychiatric or a peer review committee, but we should know that the presence of any one of the three "D's" is enough to turn on the caution lights! Remember the famous quote of Abraham Lincoln – *"This too shall pass."*

"And the rewards of stock market success are among the most satisfactory and the most valuable that may be hoped for, either as a direct business or as a part-time hobby. For those rewards consist not only in financial remuneration but extend far deeper into the personal satisfaction that comes from having expended time, study and individual effort in the mastery of a difficult and intricate science."

R. W. Schabacker—"Stock Market Theory and Practice," 1930

Discipline – Essential for Trading Success

What does discipline have to do with trading? Simply stated, trading is all about managing risks. Only a person who takes risks can be free. The key is to take risks when they are manageable; not when the risk can lead to catastrophic consequences.

Being disciplined in your trading can make these risks manageable and exciting and in the process give you the ultimate gift – freedom! Freedom from worrying about your trading because you are now disciplined to think in terms of probabilities and risk control. Making discipline a daily habit allows you "to weave a habit of a strand a day of discipline until this cable of discipline is almost unbelievable."

Discipline in trading presents itself in several parts: First, there is the preparation. Trading is simple but it ain't easy, to quote an old market axiom. Many hours of preparation occur long before any trade is entered. Here are the steps of preparation:

1. *Mental* – think through what risks are present in the trade. Knowing how to get out of the trade is very important. Mental preparation assumes that no alcohol is consumed from Sunday through Thursday of the trading week. Alcohol damages brain cells and may take up to 24 hours to completely leave your blood stream.
2. *Technical* – this varies by the methodology used by each trader. All trading opportunities should be explored. A daily ritual of scanning charts will present many good opportunities. This is the time consuming part of trading.
3. *Physical* – take time to do some type of exercise like golf, tennis or walking. It will release tension, stress, and pamper your heart.

Discipline is also necessary on the execution side of trading. Risk control is the most critical element of the trading process. Never forget how a devastating loss destroys your "psyche". It damages the trader's soul.

Monitoring a profitable trade in progress also requires discipline – you must follow the trading plan. Don't be concerned about the little fluctuations if your goal is higher. Ask yourself these questions: Has the market changed since I placed the trade? Can I afford the risk on this trade? If the answer to both of these questions is yes, then you must stay in the trade.

These brief examples highlight the important role of discipline in the life of a trader. It is truly essential in helping the trader prepare, execute and manage their positions.

"...A reasonable man should not jeopardize the capital of a trading account until he has proved to his own satisfaction, by paper-trading, that he has mastered the art. Then he is ready to start in a small way, to take the risk of actual trading. If he then proves that he can hurdle the psychological barrier of trading with real money, he is on the road to profits in the stock market."

H. M. Gartley—
"Profits in the Stock Market," 1935

Discipline is the Foundation of Freedom

Trading is all about discipline. Discipline to take the trade, and more importantly to take the loss when necessary. There is no greater feeling in the trading world than waking each morning knowing that your methodology is capable of beating the market. The key word here is "capable". All trading methodologies are based on probability not certainty! If you possess the necessary discipline to follow a profitable methodology it can lead you to freedom – the freedom to make as much money as you need; work at a profession you love; and the freedom to do what you want to do! Discipline is a two part process:

1) Preparation and
2) Execution

Preparation for trading is an ongoing process. It should become a habit! *"A habit is built by a strand a day until it becomes almost unbreakable."* – Napoleon Hill! Ethical work habits are the foundation of all successful businesses. Trading is no exception.

Preparation is three fold. First, there is the mental preparation. Knowing your methodology is tantamount to this preparation. Each day I read a few pages of Mark Douglas's book "Trading in the Zone", prior to the start of trading. This functions as an anchor for my day to remind me to think in probabilities.

The second part of preparation is the technical. Knowing what you're going to trade requires homework. I am a pattern recognition trader and routinely follow about eighty stocks, in addition to the major stock indices, currencies and Treasury Bonds. Each pattern has its own probability of success. Each pattern has its own measurement of risk control. These patterns must be categorized before the opening of the next days trading. Only eight to ten of these patterns may complete each day and of those only four to five may be tradable, but these are your "bread and butter" trades!

The third part of preparation is physical. Adequate rest, a good diet, and physical exercise contribute greatly to trading success. A word of caution here - I highly recommend that you consume no alcohol from Sunday through Friday trading. Alcohol destroys brain cells! It is just not worth it to drink during the trading week!

Preparation is followed by execution as the foundation for discipline. The mixture of the execution process is risk control and profit protection. Risk is the only thing we can control in the trading process. We can "never" know which trades are going to work. Nor can we "ever" know how much we are going to make on a trade. This leaves the only thing we can control – risk. *"He who knows not what he risks – risks it all."*

Profit protection requires monitoring the price action in order to reduce risk as soon as possible. Once a trade begins to work, it is a good money management process to reduce the risk in the trade. We deal in probabilities in trading. If you control your risk on the trade, the probability of getting a winning streak is increased. If you don't control your risk, the probability of ruin is certain.

"He who knows not what he risks, risks all."
John Hill—Founder Commodity Research Institute

Do What is Good

If only all religions would base their belief on these two statements our world would be very close to freedom from wars, hatred, anti-Semitism and apartheid all over the world.

Trading is not like religion unless you count all the investors praying that their position will turn around and get them back to even. Trading is about doing the right thing! Sometimes doing the right thing hurts in the short run but it eases the pain in the long term. Doing what is good in trading relates to minimizing your exposure to risk. Believing in yourself and your trading methodology is a very close second. But it is still in second place because risk control is the most important factor in speculation.

Traders that make it to the professional level have made the adjustments necessary to take their trading to the next level. This process continues forever because trading is a journey – not a destination. All of us are on the same journey and we all strive to make our trading flawless.

"Since the beginning of time, man has largely been controlled by emotions, fear and greed. When a student of market action allows these emotions to influence his market response, he loses many opportunities in the market. The student must at all times resist these two emotions. Confidence and courage are required to overcome fear and greed. Courage is inborn. Confidence is gained by study, study, and more study."

John Hill

Founder Commodity Research Institute

Do What is Right—Believe What is Real

This business of speculator is similar to every other business. Rules apply on the operation of the business that has been time proven over hundreds of years. Unfortunately, these rules a speculator has are not found formally in any course. Most are found fragmented throughout the many books that have been published.

Let's look at trading at its most basic level. We buy things in hope they go up—We short things in anticipation of them going down so we can cover them at a lower price. No problem here. But you must do what is right and that is to limit the loss on what you buy. If you owned a hardware store and bought a large supply of lawn mowers and soon found out they were not the good quality you had thought, wouldn't it seem logical to drop the price or get a rebate from the manufacturer? The storeowner would cut his losses and move to the next promotion. This is the right thing to do. Capital will be freed for new promotions and the pain of looking at an investment gone bad.

"Take care of your losses, and the profits will take care of themselves."

—Amos B. Hostetter

Believing what is real is the engine that will keep you going. The sound marketing plan or trading plan accompanied by excellent money management, and good execution of the plan, will be the foundation of your success in business. One good purchase of lawn mowers is of no consequence in the long run. Business is based on probabilities of certain outcomes and the inherent risks associated with those outcomes. You must have confidence in your game plan.

As one of my favorite mentors used to drill into me each day, *"Don't ever go for broke because you just might succeed!"*

"Perhaps my number one rule is: Don't try to make a profit on a bad trade, just try to find the best way to get out."
Linda Bradford Raschke

Don't be a Nail

There is an Old Persian proverb that states that *"the nail that is sticking up is the one that gets hammered down."* The analogy you can draw to the markets is over confidence and egotism. Nothing can humble you as fast as a wrong opinion of yourself and of the markets. Humility is a most noble trait as a trader. It will help you hold your perspective and allow you the flexibility of being wrong and knowing that you are wrong. There is a big difference in being wrong and knowing that you are wrong. When you know that you are wrong you are in perfect position to do something about it. It is much better to be wrong for the right reason than being right for the wrong reason. The latter situation is a disaster waiting to hap pen.

During the early 70's I was trading from a Conti Commodity office in Los Angeles which would be the trading home for no less than 5 of the original market wizards as described by Jack Schwager in his 'Market Wizards' book. Each of these successful traders had the essence of humility surrounding them. It took a devastating loss to bring me to my knees. The loss was so great that it forced me to stop trading for almost two years. It was those two years that allowed me to learn what I had done right and what the errors of past trading mistakes were. I've always loved the quote from legendary soybean trader Roy Longstreet, *"Your first mistake teaches but the second mistake kills."* Usually the first mistake is a bad trade. The second mistake is in not doing something about it (like using a stop loss order).

"The creation of a speculator's wealth comes from how he manages his money, not some magical, mysterious system or alchemist's secret. Successful investing makes money; successful investing with proper money management can create immense wealth."

Larry Williams—
"The Right Stock at the Right Time"

Ebb and Flow

Trading is extremely "easy" when you get the direction right! It is a flow and rhythm you can feel when you catch a move.

When you are going the wrong way, (opposite direction the market is moving, and it is still traveling to IT'S destination, as opposed to yours) it can feel a bit like driving your car into a cement wall.

It's the same in skiing. Brian, my ski instructor, was teaching me some technical aspects of skiing moguls, otherwise known as "bumps." We stood on top of a mogul run and looking down at the maze of bumps and wondering which way to go to get down, Brian had me imagine what path water would take if he took a bucket of water and poured it down the hill. He told me the water would seek the path of least resistance and it would ebb and flow *effortlessly* down through the mogul field.

When you have the right direction in a trade it is exactly the same feeling as that image of water flowing effortlessly down the mogul run.

"It never is your thinking that makes big money, it's the sitting."
Jesse Livermore

EDUCATING YOUR PSYCHE

Years ago technical analysis was frowned upon and looked at as "Voodoo". As time went by and technology advanced it became widely accepted and is now "mainstream".

One area emerging in the trading world but not yet mainstream is "Mental Analysis" or psychological training for traders simply put - coaching. Teaching traders how to re-focus their emotions and use them to benefit them in their trading. Trading is performance bases business as are sports. Many athletes including the world's best use coaches to help them get through mental blocks and excel in their field.

An individual trader can study technical and fundamental approaches for years. These areas of study literally have no end. But what about studying a mental approach to trading? An approach that gives the trader a plan for the mental aspect of trading including implementing mental stops. It's no secret that once a good technical or fundamental approach is learned trading is 90% mental. It is also worth noting that the overwhelming majority of traders do not succeed, not because of method but because of failing to learn the correct mental approach to successfully execute a strategy.

Traders use monetary stops to limit risk and protect capital but how many traders have a plan for mental stops? An indicator, so to speak, that will alert the trader they are close to letting one or more emotions take control of their trading. Any emotion taking control in trading has the potential to do serious damage both monetarily and psychologically. Misguided emotions in trading can lead to overtrading, impulsive or compulsive trading, revenge trading, overlooking money management such as not using stops or too large of a position size, sloppy entries or simply the trader freezes and does not enter the trade. Other emotional links include being glued to minute to minute account balance fluctuations, using stops that are too tight and early exits. The list goes on. A trader **must** learn to protect their psyche just as much as their capital.

These emotionally based trading errors have nothing to do with theoretically knowing how to properly execute and manage a trade and everything to do with underlying mis-directed emotions.

Emotions are part of being human. It is not realistic or necessarily the best solution to try and remove them or ignore them, which is likely to have negative consequences and possibly trigger negative trading patterns. Instead it is more effective to learn to recognize the emotions that negatively affect trading and learn to re-organize those emotions in a manner that they will become team players for you. Work for you, not against you.

So how do you do this? How do you start to learn to re-focus and re-organize these emotions? One process to consider is working with a trading coach. A good trading coach can help to recognize the emotions responsible for negative trading patterns and then work to establish new positive patterns. The trader must, of course, do some work to accomplish this. Think about this, just one negative pattern in trading can keep a trader from reaching their potential!

An important technique that a trading coach would instill is methods to employ mental stops. A way for the trader to stop trading before serious damage is done.

Traders spend a lot of time and money investing in learning a good method of trading that suits their personality. It is my belief that time and money should also be spent learning to manage emotions in trading. Hopefully someday this will be looked at as a natural part of learning to trade. Just as learning technical analysis is today. The mental aspect of trading can not be separated out and learning good solid techniques will only improve the skill of the trader. You can not have one without the other.

"There is only one side to the stock market and it is not the Bull side or the Bear side, but the Right side."
Jesse Livermore

Eliminating Fear

In trading, fear is one of the most common and difficult obstacles to overcome. Fear is so much stronger than greed! You can actually see the physical signs of fear – the sweating, agitation, chalk white around the mouth, white knuckles, etc. I suppose this is why the movie industry produces so many horror films because fear can be measured.

On the other hand, there are not many films on greed, are there? The funny thing about fears is that the vast majority never come true. They exist in our minds only. Trading with fear can be used as a great equalizer because the trader should focus on the amount of money at risk on any trading situation. Roy Longstreet used to comment, *"I'm running scared and loving it."*

When facing these fears, and we must face them, it might be good to ask the question "what is the worst thing that could happen?" If the pain in the answer to this question is too much to bear then simply exit the trade. The main reason traders' exit their losers is that the pain of losing one more dollar becomes almost unbearable. All of this pain could be eliminated by using a trading plan and learning to think in probabilities – nothing is certain. We should all remember that we are going to die and in the long run of life, trading is truly insignificant.

There are two quotes that I use when I mentor students on trading.

"All men die but most men never live." Trading is very emotional and if you use this emotional experience as a life enhancing process it can be exhilarating. This is especially true after a series of winning trades or one monster win. Each day in trading is unique to all others. My personal definition of "hell" is going to a job each day and counting the hours, minutes and seconds during the day. Confucius said a man who enjoys his work is on a permanent vacation. The second quote is;

"A coward dies a thousand deaths but a brave man just one." Why worry about things that we have no control over? We all die in the end! If you have fear and pain in your trading, then it is not for you. Do something else because it is not worth damaging your mental and physical health.

Fear can be overcome but you must find the source and face it head on. Above all, "To thine ownself be true"!

"The single most important reason that people lose money in the financial markets is that they don't cut their losses short. It is a curiosity of human nature that no matter how many books talk about this rule, and no matter how many experts offer this advice, people still keep making the same mistake."
Victor Sperandeo

Faith Is the Other Side of Doubt

Knowing that your methodology can "beat" or outperform the market is a great feeling. This does not mean you win every day. However, probability is on your side. A slight edge used with sound money management can yield consistent returns. But you have to believe in your methodology! You must know you can win! This reminds me of one of my favorite poems:

If you think you are beaten – you are
If you think to dare not – you won't
If you would like to win but think you can't
It's almost a cinch you won't
Life's battles don't always go to the
stronger or faster man
But sooner or later the man who wins
Is the one who thinks he can!

Nothing is more important than a positive mental approach to the process of trading – "Altitude is determined by Attitude." Read books that focus on positive affirmations. Some of my personal favorite affirmations are:

1) You can do it if you think you can.
2) My first mistake teaches – My second mistake kills.
3) Success is measured not by the number of successes but by picking yourself up after each failure and starting again.
4) As the mind thinks – so it is!
5) You can only fail if you stop trying.
6) There are no losers just those that quit trying.
7) Success is 90% perspiration and 10% inspiration

Preparing yourself mentally in a positive way will improve your trading results. It will not happen overnight – it will be an ongoing process but the results will be etched in your "psyche." It is then that your subconscious takes over and it becomes part of your trading armor.

"I can say that after years of studying traders, the best predictor of success is simply whether the person is improving with time and experience. Many traders unconsciously acknowledge their lack of progress by continually jumping from one system or methodology to another, never gaining true proficiency in any. As a result, these people end up with one year of experience six times instead of six years of experience."
Charles Faulkner

FEAR

F.E.A.R. is false evidence appearing real! Seldom do our fears materialize. The popular talk show psychologist, Dr. Phil recently shared some insight into the process of fear and phobias. He categorized fear into two segments, rational fears (the ones that could happen) and the irrational fears (those that almost never happen and are disproportionate to logic).

Rational fears are our body's defense mechanism for our survival, i.e., walking across a heavily trafficked street. Irrational fears are the source of most of our misery. Plane crashes, disease, and poverty fall into this category of the never-ending family of phobias.

There are three things you can do to help overcome the threat of fear;

1. Differentiate between the rational and irrational fear, if it isn't life threatening it is probably irrational fear.

2. Ask yourself this question, what is the worst thing that could happen if the fear becomes real? The answer is usually so absurd that it brings you to the realization that it doesn't matter anyway. We are all going to die! Don't live your life in fear. All men die—Some men never live.

3. Think of only positive thoughts that come into your mind. The use of 3x5 index cards with positive affirmations is an easy and extremely effective exercise toingrain positive thoughts into your psyche.

Your trading will improve immensely if you keep your Thoughts on the positive side of your psyche!

"Consistent winners tell virtually no one their activities in the marketplace...Consistent losers tell anyone who will listen the details of their market activities, to the point of campaigning for their point of view."
Henry Clasing

Fear and Responsibility

Law Enforcement personnel are trained to be extremely careful of one particular type of suspect. The person that has nothing to lose is the most dangerous of all animals. Backed against the wall they will muster every conceivable trick to survive.

It is this mind set that you need to be successful. You are at your best when you have nothing else to lose. All of your progress moves forward from this point.

"Just do it" as the athletic shoe ad extols. How true it is! Each journey must begin with the first step and trading is a journey, not a destination!

Focus on the process of doing the next thing to insure your survival. Forget the excuses. We all can make excuses but we can't find one reason why we can't succeed! It boils down to one thing – responsibility. The freedom that comes with trading carries some baggage. That baggage is taking responsibility for all of the decisions – the good and the bad! Only when we step up to the plate to play in the great trading game and realize that it is only you who carries the bat will you realize the importance of responsibility.

"Repeatedly...I have sold a stock while it still was rising—and that has been one reason why I have held onto my fortune. Many a time, I might have made a good deal more by holding a stock, but I would also have been caught in the fall when the price of the stock collapsed."
Bernard Baruch

Finding a Way Out

Some of my most relaxing moments are watching old television series especially the detective programs such as Mannix, The Rockford Files and Banacek. Along with the movies it offers me an escape from the long day of trading. Occasionally there will be a very poignant message hidden in the script of these melodramas.

One of my favorites came from a line by Robert Dinero in the movie 'Ronin'. A. Ronin is a Japanese samurai who is selected to fight to the death to protect his master. During the dialogue Dinero declares, "I will never enter a room until I can determine that there are at least two ways out of it!" Trading should be approached in a similar manner. Don't focus on how much you might make on a trade but rather focus on how much you may lose on the transaction. Winners think – how much can I lose – Losers think – how much can I make. Next time you are in Las Vegas take a look at the flashy signs and promise of big payoffs. Find the big slot machine that promises millions if you can line up four diamonds in a row! Now find the slot machine that states boldly "This machine has taken in 10 million dollars this year and paid out 2 million." Lots of luck – it won't be found.

When you put on a trade be sure that your trading plan includes the exit strategy you desire. Besides using a stop order, try using a time stop! A time stop relates to the time you have been in a position. For example, you have been in a trade for three days and have not been stopped out of the position but it is still losing a small amount. Exit the position on the open of the fourth day and re-evaluate your reasoning behind the trade. If I were a betting man, it would probably be the best thing to do in almost all of these situations.

"...it is just that this game, where like any performance oriented discipline, it is easy to be very critical of ourselves, for not playing the piece perfectly, for picking apart our game...you HAVE to take pressure off yourself and look at the small amount of progress you gradually make. The FIRST step in a trader's education is simply learning to control emotions and be as objective as possible."

Linda Bradford Raschke

Freedom

Trading is one of the few endeavors that allow you the ultimate in freedom. Freedom as it relates to time, expression and monetary goals! The problem many traders face is that they are not prepared to accept the responsibility that is associated with this new found freedom. Most of us are destined to lead highly structured lives, usually working for someone else. One of my mentors once gave me his description of hell – "working a nine to five job that you hated for a boss you hated even more." All of us have probably been in that position at least once in our lives.

Trading successfully takes us to a new level of life's enjoyable moments. We decide when we work, what we do, who we deal with and the hours we chose to expend. Within my group of trading buddies lies a similar theme! The love what they do and the hours are not counted. Their motto is – "Thank God it's Monday" not the usual, "Thank God it's Friday." Weekends are welcome but it's the anticipation of the trading week that excites us all. Confucius said *"Find a job that you truly love and you will be on a life long vacation."* Nothing describes trading better than this statement.

Use your time and effort to arrive at that point in your trading career and your life long vacation will begin for you. One last bit of advice, don't ever give up! Success can be just a heart-beat away! Search out others who have made the journey. Most are willing to give you some good advice. Trading is a journey not a destination!

"You did what you knew how to do, and when you knew better, you did better."
Maya Angelou

Go With the Edge

Many people who have no knowledge of trading make the assumption that it is nothing more than gambling. But usually their definition of gambling is someone who takes unnecessary risks with money who have little chance of getting anything back monetarily and possess no personal discipline.

Although there are similarities between trading and gambling there are some very important distinctions as well. There are professional gamblers that have studied mathematically how they would have an edge if they optimally played a given game over a period of time that would allow them to have an outcome of financially gaining. Then there are gamblers who plan on taking a certain amount of their hard earned income and "win or lose" plan on blowing it all at a gambling facility adding to the lovely decors of those facilities. Trading also has participants from both sides of this coin. But let's for the sake of this article assume that the gambling participant and the trader both have knowledge of how their games work. I will use the game of blackjack as the gambling example here.

Here are some important distinctions between the two:

The bets – In blackjack your bet is placed *before* the player has any idea of the probability of winning against the dealer. The total bet is the total risk unlike trading futures, commodities or stocks. Just think of this, if you could place your bet *after* your hand is dealt and the dealers up card is showing, do you think that might improve the outcome of the game for you?

In trading your bet is placed when it has been determined that you have an edge in the game and the probability of winning is on your side.

The exits - In blackjack once your bet is placed you **can not** take back any portion of it. You will win, lose it all, or push. If you see you have a high percentage of winning the hand against the dealer you can not increase your bet. There is no point at which you can take partial profits.

In trading once your bet is placed you have the option of limiting the amount of capital lost through stop loss protection, reducing the size of the bet. You can take partial profits, adding on if the trade moves in your favor or exit at a break even.

The distinction of not entering a trade until the odds favor you gives you a tremendous edge in trading, the ability to control the risk. Also being able to vary the bet by increasing it or reducing it at the appropriate times are differences that greatly impact the outcome. There are methods to make a decision to play or not play at a particular table in blackjack but not nearly as good as knowing the percentage up front as in trading. Both are games of skill and both can have an element of luck, although I believe luck is the result of good preparation.

Although the distinctions are subtle the outcomes can be dramatic between the two. There is no substitute for good money management and the patience to wait for the right trade to come along.

"He who gains a victory over other men is strong; but he who gains a victory over himself is all powerful."
Lao-Tse

Great Books from the Past

Accumulating hundreds of thousands of dollars worth of books over five decades enabled me to examine the countless trading systems and trading ideas they contained. Most books contain *some* valuable tidbits. The joy comes from finding one that lays a foundation of understanding that enables you to grow as a trader. There are three such books in my opinion. Each will be discussed briefly. They are *not* listed in their order of importance, as I believe they are all equal. They are all thirty to sixty years old!

Profits in the Stock Market, by H.M. Gartley was published in 1938. It was the basis of a trading course in stocks. It cost $1,500.00 in 1938 (about the cost of three new automobiles). The seven hundred plus pages contain most of what the modern day technicians' use in their analysis of the stock market. But Gartley went one step further. He included stock and stock index charts from the 1800's through 1938. These charts are illustrated by swing charts, point and figure charts and bar graphs. My favorite is the 1906 – 1936 time period where you can see all swings with the date of every significant high and low. The charts are large and are worthy of framing. Pages 200-250 in Gartley's book have yielded more commercial trading systems than any other book every written such as, *The Tubb's Stock Market Course, The Trident System,* and *The Reverse Point Wave* just to name a few. Gartley's book is a must for the serious technician.

The Profit Magic of Stock Transaction Timing by James Hurst was introduced thirty years ago. His work focused on the cyclic nature of stock market cycles. Hurst explained his theories of nominal cycles, periodicity, and synchronicity and at the time it was the most widely followed trading system for commodities for several years. Hurst developed a trading course with his use of cycles and entitled it *Cycltec*. A vast number of audio cassettes and manuals were included in this course. It has some of the most interesting and useful material for those interested in cycles. Traders Press has recently re-introduced the material at a fraction of the original cost.

The last book, *The Torque Analysis of Stock Market Cycles*, by William Garrett, was also introduced thirty years ago. There were a lot of coincidences with the books at the time. Both books were written by engineers, both of the authors were traders, both books talked about cycles, and the books were issued by the same publisher. Hurst's book was easier to understand than Garrett's. The Hurst book was priced at $10.00 and the Garrett book at $30.00. Garrett's book sold only a few hundred copies but Hurst's book sold thousands.

I had a copy of the Garrett book on my bookshelf for eight years not knowing its value until one of my peers; Bryce Gilmore – developer of the Wave Trader and author of several books on market Geometry – showed me its significance. Page eighty-nine of the Garrett book illustrates the "Golden

Spiral" better than any other book of its era. In fact, it was the only book at the time that touched on the subject. It is the essence of the Elliott Wave principle in my opinion.

Bryce and I were fortunate enough to contact Clarice Garrett (the author's widow) and the book has been beautifully reproduced in leather for $100.00.

If you're serious about trading, I suggest that you add these books to your personal library. If you make a commitment to studying the material, you can build the foundation you will need to be a successful trader. Consider it an investment in yourself.

"Our doubts are traitors,
And make us lose the good we oft might win
By fearing to attempt."
William Shakespeare

GREATNESS FOLLOWS FAILURE

Most of us can only learn from our mistakes! It is only the fortunate that can bypass this process. The smart man learns from his mistakes. The wise man learns from the mistakes of others. This is why failure is so important in trading. Hopefully, we learn from each trading mistake.

General George S. Patton stated, *"You do not measure a man by his success, the true measurement of a man's character is how high he bounces after he falls down."* Children born to nurturing parents are the greatest recipients of this kind of thinking. Battered children are punished and cajoled while making their first mistakes. Traders have a tendency to act like a battered child. Constant mental bickering about; "this could have been better," or "What happened to me was so unlucky," does nothing but fester the wounds. Shake off the mistake. Move on to the next trade. Failure in trading is a necessary event. It is not evil and not meant for you alone. Failure in trading is like breathing. Failure is followed by success. The faster you learn to embrace failure the faster the footsteps of greatness will walk side by side with you.

"When you get into a tight place and everything goes against you, till it seems as though you could not hold on a minute longer, never give up then, for that is just the place and time that the tide will turn."

Harriet Beecher Stowe

Harmonic Numbers

In John Michell's fantastic book *The Dimensions of Paradise*, he illustrates the amazing harmony in all things (living and non-living). Most fascinating are the similarities in the patterns from the earth and their comparisons in astronomy. Throughout this rare book are examples of the repetition in nature. This same phenomenon is present in all actively traded stocks and commodities. It is this repetition I refer to as Harmonic numbers.

Back in the late 70's (that's 1970's) at Drexel, Burnham, Lambert, Jim Twentyman and I categorized thirty-minute price swings on gold, silver, soybeans and T-Bonds. Using a (then very fast) Wang computer we statistically examined the data for clues to price action and pattern recognition. The results were amazing! Each commodity had its own distinct vibration. I believe that this vibration is similar to the "Doppler Effect" in wave theory. The initial wave or shock ripples through a sequence of larger than smaller waves until they dissipate. Similar shock waves occur in stocks and commodities.

Harmonic or vibratory numbers can be found by following thirty-minute charts and looking for the similar price swings. All swings are related by .618, .786, 1.0, 1.27, and 1.618 but there will be one wave that repeats more than others. This will be the harmonic number or wave.

Knowing the harmonic number has several distinct advantages. First, it gives you information on how far a price move may be expected to go. Second, it can be a valuable aid in risk management and stop placement. Don't place your stop exactly where the harmonic number is expected. When day trading, the harmonic number will at times be the exact range from high to low.

To quote Jim Twentyman, *"Defy human nature – do the work yourself,"* and witness this phenomenon first hand!

"All that we are is the result of what we have thought. The mind is everything. What we think, we become."
Buddha

HOPE

Hope is a four letter word. An appropriate acronym for H.O.P.E. could be;

Having
Our
Prayers
Expected.

False hope is a great source of misery and not just in the trading arena. Prayers are always good by keeping in mind that some of Gods greatest gifts are her unanswered prayers.

Hoping is a sign that the trader has no control over his position. Traders should never be hoping and always trying to control the amount of risk at stake at all times. Always trading – never hoping should be a trader's motto.

""Finish each day and be done with it... You have done what you could; some blunders and absurdities no doubt crept in: forget them as soon as you can. Tomorrow is a new day: you shall begin it well and serenely."

Ralph Waldo Emerson

Keep Your Windows Open

There is a religious phrase echoed by many different faiths all saying pretty much the same thing – *"When your God closes a door it's because he wants you to open a window."* We all make our own destiny and the quicker we find that the responsibility is on our shoulders the quicker we can move ahead. There are no dead ends in life – only missed opportunities. And not all (in fact very few) ever turn out as we expected. The frustration of trading result from our own unfulfilled expectation of what should have happened.

One of my favorite detective series had a line that I'll always remember – *"I never enter a room until I see how I am going to get out."* Sage advice when you are in a trade don't you think? It's much better to be out of a market wishing you were in than being in a market wishing you were out! Trading plans are meant to have windows for those unforeseen events after entering the trading door. These windows will protect you form your strongest enemy – yourself!

Predetermined exit strategies help prevent the catastrophic occurrences that are present in any trade. Writings from some of the legends in trading (Livermore, Soros, and Paul Tudor Jones) and scores of others, tell harrowing tales of trading disasters.

Keep your window unlocked or even slightly open. The fresh air will not only invigorate you it might just stimulate some new thinking!

"Anyone can carry his burden, however hard, until nightfall. Anyone can do his work however hard, for one day. Anyone can live sweetly, patiently, lovingly, purely, til the sun goes down. And this is all that life really means."
Robert Louis Stevenson

Keeping Promises

There is no promise harder to keep than the promise you make with yourself. Rationalizing in our minds about the promise allows our mind to change the promise or forget about it altogether. There is an old saying in the teaching of the Buddha – *"I shall keep the promise that I make to myself."*

Two key words are of tantamount importance in this saying – promise and myself. A promise is a contract. In this instance you are acting as both parties in the contract. It's just you and your subconscious. No one should know of the promise except the parties involved – You!

The second key word in the sentence is myself. Make the promise work for you. Do the things that work and don't do the things that don't work. Keep the promise to yourself simple and easy to remember. One promise at a time. If there are too many components in the promise it becomes confusing. Confusion leads to non-fulfillment of the promise.

A promise made to yourself should be both very simple and very sacred. Prayer is probably the closest analogy that can be made for this process. In prayer, we ask the almighty for guidance and help. Most often our prayers seem as though the Almighty is not listening. Some of God's greatest gifts are unanswered prayers. These unanswered prayers can truly be a blessing in disguise because we must now get the answers on our own.

"It is no disgrace to start all over. It is usually an opportunity."
George Matthews Adams

Know When to Hold Them and When to Fold Them

It is a given that traders cannot win 100 percent of the time, because with reward comes risk, and losses are as much a fact of life as taxes and death. But there are highly valuable lessons to be learned about the trading process that go far beyond the dollar signs. How traders put reliable steps in place to ensure that their performance may be enhanced on the road to success is critical. And, for most, success is dependent not only on what is done correctly but, also, on what potentially havoc-wreaking mistakes can be avoided.

The three practical principals that can aid in anticipating and possibly avoiding mistakes are probability, self-discipline and responsibility – simple enough to write, but harder to carry out.

No successful trader would deny that mental preparation is just as necessary as charts and market signals. Trading is all about probabilities and, while every trader encounters a losing streak or draw down of equity, success as a trader is measured by how well losses are handled mentally.

A "sure" sign of potential disaster is holding large losses in open positions while at the same time taking many small profits. This is contrary to the market adage by a wise trader/mentor from Commodity Corporation, Amos Barr Hostetter, who said, *"Take care of your losses and your profits will take care of themselves."* A trader who mentally dupes himself into believing that the small profits will offset the large losses is taking a dangerous ostrich approach.

Most losing streaks are the result of probability distribution. In 100 trades, a system should encounter a losing streak of up to eight trades in a row, and this is the time when the trader begins to question the validity of the system. It also normally is the worst time to stop trading as long as the trader has followed his methodology, because it's been shown that winning streaks generally follow losing streaks.

Examining daily trading logs enables the trader to spot some common trading mistakes such as lack of discipline, sloppiness in trade preparation, impulse trading, impatience, and all of the other cousins and uncles in the "mistake family." One of the big advantages of the pattern recognition method of swing trading is the probability associated with each pattern. Winning is a matter of executing all of the trades as the patterns develop.

Traders must train themselves to think in terms of probability for three very important reasons:

1. No one knows with 100-percent certainty whether the trade will be profitable or not.
2. No one knows how much money will be made or lost on a trade.
3. If the trader does not control the profit outcome and

does not know with 100-percent certainty which trades will work, then the trader should spend 100 percent of his time concentrating on the only element of the trade he *can* control – the risk of the trade.

Key to success is the ability to pinpoint how much one can afford to lose. Winners think "how much can I lose?" Losers think "how much can I win?" This fact is easy to demonstrate. Anyone visiting Las Vegas – has been greeted by brightly colored, flashing slot machines that beckon the full-pocketed tourist with the promise "Win One Million Dollars!" However, no visitor has ever seen a sign that reads, "This machine has taken in three million dollars this year." When the trader truly learns how to think like the "house" the probability of winning is increased.

Thinking about losing requires discipline. By focusing acutely on a trading plan, the probabilities for profits or losses and streaks of each, and risk control, risk – taking becomes more manageable and can give traders the ultimate gift – freedom. In fact, making discipline a daily habit allows traders "to weave a habit of a strand a day of discipline until the cable of discipline is almost unbelievable."

Discipline in trading presents itself in several parts. First, there is preparation. Trading is simple, but it takes time. Many hours of preparation occur *long before* any trade is entered. These steps include:

Mental – Traders must think through what risks are present in the trade, and know in advance how to get out of the trade and at what point. Mental preparation, from my experience, also assumes eliminating alcohol consumption from Sunday through Thursday of the trading week, because it typically takes up to 24 hours to completely leave the blood system. It's best to have the brain working at an optimal level.

Technical – Methodologies vary by the individual trader. All trading opportunities should be explored. A daily ritual of scanning charts will present many good *opportunities.* This is the time consuming part of trading. Opportunities, however, do not guarantee profits.

Physical – Traders need to release tension in a positive way. Take time to do some type of exercise like golf, tennis or walking.

Discipline is also necessary on the execution side of trading. Risk control is the most critical element of the trading process. Never forget how a devastating loss can destroy the "psyche." It damages the trader's soul.

Monitoring a profitable trade in progress also requires discipline – follow the trading plan. Do not be concerned about minuscule fluctuations if your goal is higher. There are two questions that every trader should ask: "Has the market changed since I placed the trade? Can I afford to take the risk on this trade?" If the answer to both of these questions is "yes", the trader should stay in the trade.

Along with discipline, responsibility plays a significant role in the trading game. Once in the market, the trader alone has responsibility for his or her trading decisions – no one else. Not assuming personal responsibility is like jumping into a fast-moving river without a life jacket in the hopes that there is a lifeguard somewhere on the shore. The trader can keep afloat only if he is responsible for his won destiny. Take joy in the good decisions and learn from the bad ones. Place the orders, close the orders and take the profits. Or, swallow hard, and take the loss if that's the responsible thing to do and your plan points in that direction.

Traders can and do fall into the habit of making excuses about why something went wrong. Again quoting Hostetter, *"Forget your profits, but forget your losses faster."*

Taking responsibility can be improved by including a few steps or reminders in the trading plan. What works for one trader might not work for another. The way to handle this is to place a written statement on the computer. The statement says: "Has the pattern in the trade changed from the original pattern? Has the initial price objective been reached?" If the answer to both of these questions is "yes", it's time to exit the trade. If the answer is "no", then the trade must continue. Trading is a business of dealing with probabilities, *not certainties.* Hostetter held that, *"We never know which trades will work – the problem arises when we only 'think' we know."*

Probability, discipline and responsibility are traits that every trader should strive to attain. Probability assures that losing streaks will develop just as winning streaks will. What matters is how to recover from those losses. Discipline and responsibility help to prevent devastating losses and aid in recovery. Have the discipline to exit or stay in a trade, and take responsibility for the actions and outcome. Again, losses are not 100 percent preventable; however, with the right trading strategies and mental focus, many may be avoided.

"All that is necessary to break the spell of inertial and frustration is this: Act as if it were impossible to fail. That is the talisman, the formula, the command of right-about-face which turns us from failure towards success."
Dorothea Brande

LAUGHTER

An old axiom that "Laughter is the best medicine" is equally true in trading. We must be able to laugh at our mistakes. Trading mistakes only cost us money and sometimes our pride. What an advantage over medicine where mistakes can be fatal!

Laughter does three very positive things in your life.

1.) It is impossible to be in a negative thought mood when you are laughing. 2.) It reduces tension and increases blood flow and respiration.
3.) You use far less muscles in your face when you are smiling.

Remember there is no sense in worrying about anything because we are all going to die anyway. Our happiness is determined by how well we decide to live our lives.

Happiness starts on the inside, not by external factors from the outside (like money and toys). Live your life each day in laughter and freedom from worry. Keep in mind the old Scottish proverb, *"All men die, some men never live!"*

As a youngster I can remember my father saying, *"If worrying did any good I would go over to the corner of the room and sweat blood."* He lived by that statement and my sister and I carried the message to our children.

When you really stop and think about all the negative ramifications caused by worry, it makes it logical to stay away from worrying. If you can think of one positive thing that happen if you worry – then go for it!

"Our greatest glory is not in never falling, but in rising every time we fall"
Oliver Goldsmith

Light Bulbs!

Trading requires an enormous amount of observing. Hours upon hours are spent observing price movement and looking at how price reacts and learning to recognize patterns that repeat with some degree of probability.

Many times a trader will have an idea lurking below the surface of something they are observing in price patterns or behavior. The idea may not quite be to the surface yet where it can be articulated and defined. It's a subtle feeling, like déjà vu, you've seen it before but not quite sure what to do with it.

Reading and studying books and magazine articles and listening to other traders, especially ones that have been in the markets for many years that have vast amounts of information to share can help trigger those ideas. Sometimes you might come across something from one of these traders that set off an entire chain of thought process for you. Maybe you have been noticing a particular price pattern but had no idea what to do with it and now you find yourself reading or hearing an exact description of what you had been seeing! It rings a bell, light bulbs go off and your creativity is engaged. It may just give you enough information to test what you have been seeing and determine if there is enough of an edge to form a trading plan. That information is now part of your trading repertoire and becomes a stepping stone. It pushes you to yet another level of trading that you weren't at the day before. And that is an exciting part of the journey!

"No one is ever beaten unless he gives up the fight."
W. Beran Wolfe

Living in the Now

There is no better way to live your life than to live it as if you have only a few days left. Enjoy the now moment because it's all we really have. This does not mean to imply you act with reckless abandon! Absolutely not. It just means to enjoy what is happening now in your life and in your trading.

Trading is such an exciting business and may add much more enjoyment in your life. But the key lies in how you look at your drinking glass. It should always look ¾ full, not half empty. Accentuate the positives in your life and trading. I see more sadness among traders I meet because they cannot muster even one slight positive thought. How sad this truly is.

What a great feeling it is when you can awaken each trading day with the knowledge that you are fully capable of beating the market almost every day. This can be done by understanding yourself first and your trading plan second. You are the wind and the sails of your trading ship. Energy must be developed and stored for your trading opportunities.

Remember, God has given us only a short amount of time on this earth to enjoy and accomplish the important things in life. She has told us that "yesterday" is now history, "tomorrow" still remains a mystery and that is why she calls it the "present". Unwrap each present with care as it may be your last!

"Rule 5: If you do make a mistake, correct it as soon as you can.
If you do make a mistake, correct yourself at the next available opportunity in the hand. Don't just keep throwing in good money after bad. There's no reason you have to follow your original mistake with additional bets. Some players feel, having made the original bad call, that they are now obligated to stay until the end in order "to be consistent," so they continue to put in more and more money behind it. Get out."

Larry W. Phillips— "The Tao of Poker"

Losers Like to Whine

"Losers like to whine about their past."

Sean Connery

This quote by Mr. 007 himself is from a line in the movie "The Rock." *"Losers focus on results – Winners focus on execution."* Losers think how much can I win. Winners focus on how much can I lose.

A good example of this principle, "It's not what you think – it's how you think", can be seen in Las Vegas. Slot machines are built with flashing lights and shrill noises to get players attention. Each machine proudly boasts how much money you can win. Look for the slot machine that says "I've taken in 1.5 million this year." This will never happen. Losers want to win but their thinking is reversed. They must learn to think in terms of risk per trade and the probability of a win. This is where a trading plan can reverse the whining about past trades and convert the trader to the positive expectation of trading. Two things are always true in speculation;

1. *No one knows with 100% certainty what is going to happen next.*
2. *The trader never knows how much profit is in the trade.*

If the trader will focus on the risk in the trade and not the profit he will increase his probability of success many fold. This concept eluded me for many years. It wasn't until my daughter (age 7) was helping me with my charts one evening. I had her look at a Sugar chart and asked her where it was going. She said higher! This exercise was repeated through the whole Commodity Perspective chart book Laren was right every time! I realized then that I didn't need to know where a market was going but where I was going to enter or exit.

"Take care of your losses and your profits will take care of themselves." – Amos Barr Hostetter, founder Commodity Corporation

"Rule 18: Take the long view.
While you'd like to win in the short term in poker (in other words, today), what you really want is to win over the long term. Ideally, you want to end up with a poker history that includes both wins and losses, with the wins dominating.
The worst thing that can befall you in poker is to be winning in today's game using a strategy that fails over the long-term."
Larry W. Phillips— "The Tao of Poker"

MISTAKES

Many of you are laboring under the false assumption that I never make mistakes, I always make money, and I never have a period where they don't go exactly as I expected. Trust me on this one! We are all alike. Trading is a journey not a destination. Everything we believe is based on probabilities. Nothing more – nothing less.

I battle the psychological trading demons every day just like I always have and all the traders before me. Each day I read five pages of Mark Douglas' book *Trading in the Zone.* This accomplishes two things – it makes me think in probabilities and second it reminds me that I have no idea what the market is going to do.

All of us carry unwanted baggage when we trade. It's because we are human. Knowing that you carry baggage is what is important. Awareness that we have weaknesses is what allows you to protect yourself from your greatest enemy – you!

There is an old Chinese proverb that is my favorite. *"The man who knows his enemy is strong but the man who knows himself is omnipotent."* Lao Tse – circa 600 BC.

No one can make money every day or every week or every month. If they did they would own the world in less than twenty years. What we strive for as traders is the ability to believe in your own methodology and learn to think in probabilities. The tide is always at its lowest when it begins to change.

I laugh at myself when I get phone calls from subscribers and students who say "if only I could trade like you." Believe me when I say – "You do, you do!"

The great New York Yankees catcher, Yogi Berra summed it up the best – *"You've gotta dance with the girl you brung to the dance."*

Remember the words of Sir Winston Churchill's most famous speech at the depth of WWII as London was under attack every night from the Nazi bombers. As he addressed the graduating class of Westminster College the great Statesman spoke these famous words – *"Never give up, Never, Never, Never,"* and he quietly left the stage!

*"**Rule 19: the goal of poker is not to win money, it is to play your cards right.** Many players believe that the goal in poker is to win money. Actually, the goal is to make a series of correct decisions. This is the real goal. Keep your focus on this and the rest will follow naturally. Correct play on each card and each hand is your real goal as a poker player."*

Larry W. Phillips— "The Tao of Poker"

Market Threshold or Market Watershed

(Written October 8, 2002)

The week of October 7th – 11th is going to be a benchmark low or acceleration point for stocks. We must watch the next two trading days October 7th and 8th very carefully due to the fragile nature of the stock market. The month of September and October have historically been associated with seasonal lows but it is never known if the low is the low for the year. What is known however is a very good trading opportunity is probably at hand this coming week in the stock market. The news is secondary to the action in the stock market. News follows the trend so expect bearish news. Watch how the market action confirms the news. If prices don't break with bearish news, odds will favor a rally. The market has been oversold for months and may continue for some time to come.

We will keep a close eye on stock market conditions and alert you as the situation warrants.

The financial stocks and the banking index are at precarious points on the charts! Look at the chart of JPM. This once prestigious firm has been under attack and is resting at the 1.618 expansion of the last major swing. Remember recent charts of AOL, F, WCOM and a host of others that dropped off by 50% or more once the 1.618 level failed to hold.

The second week in October is probably the most critical time period for the stock market since the top of March 2000 when all the patterns were screaming “sell the farm and go short.” Needless to say we will watch the next few days closely!

As of today, October 8th, the markets tested the lows of July. These lows must hold. If they are violated it will not be good for stocks.

Also keep an eye on the banking indexes and stocks related, such as JPM, GS and MWD. These also must hold the lows here.

Today was the last day of the + (-) two days of the new moon cycle.

"The dollar you keep from losing on a losing day is the same dollar you add to a win on a winning day."
Mike Caro

METAMORPHOSIS

Just as the butterfly evolves from the caterpillar's cocoon, traders make changes throughout their careers. Some changes are brought about by the volatility of the markets (or lack of volatility).

Isaac Newton and Thomas Edison were two giants of intellect that thrived on change. Newton's favorite work was the sculpture of the Chambered Nautilus. He was so infatuated by it that he had it engraved on the headboard of his oak bed. That headboard can be seen at Wellesley College outside of Boston.

Change never stops. It is in fact the only thing that never stops. Everything in the Universe is constantly expanding or contracting. But there are things that each of us can do to make changing as painless as possible.

First – learn to enjoy the change! No one wants to be mired in a monotonous environment. Take a lesson from an old adage, *"Yesterday is history, tomorrow is a mystery, so every-*

day is a present." Unwrap the present day gift with anticipation. Remember life is like a salad, it can be chicken salad or chicken s—t! It all depends on what we put in it!

Second – develop the desire to want the things you want and develop the trust in yourself to accept that you are truly deserving of these things.

Look at how much your life has changed over the years. The only time we will stop changing is when our hearts finally stop beating. Why not learn to enjoy the process of change!

"One of the keys to successful trading is to get in tune with your own investment psychology. That is, you can never be as successful trading according to other people's ideas and trigger points as you can trading according to your own."
Michael S. Shopshire, Ph.D.—
"The Winning Trader, Developing a Mental Edge for Market Success"

Mindset of the Neophyte Trader

It is becoming more widespread in thought that the successful trader possesses a mindset that is unique and different than that of the struggling trader. I think that is without question. But some food for thought for the novice trader. What type of mindset is necessary for someone who wants to learn to trade, and learn to trade consistently and successfully? What type of mindset will most benefit the novice?

First of all there must be a very strong desire to learn trading. I also believe that it is imperative that the novice be independent in their thinking process. If you look at the profession of trading and take into account that very few succeed, that should in itself give a clue as to what may be needed.

The overwhelming majority of novice trader's are simply looking for an easy solution to trading. Something they don't have to work at but will make them a lot of money fast. Most will not admit that they will never put in the appropriate time or money into their education. They would simply like to read a book or two and then call themselves a trader. Some will spend some money on a program or methodology but the expectations are not realistic and will soon either blame the program or the creator of the method and simply say it doesn't work.

Now let's get into what type of mindset is going to allow the novice trader to learn the necessary ingredients of trading that will ultimately account for their success or failure. The mindset of the student must be open for starters. This means that the student must be willing to assume full responsibility for his or her own process, and the student must always look deeper for the answers. They must be willing to go through periods of frustration and exasperation. That is part of any learning process. Their ability to observe the markets and price movement and translate that into opportunity is crucial. Observation is the key word here. Perseverance will go a long way in learning to trade well.

Think back through history for a moment, try and think of some great minds that advanced history in some way. They did not do it by someone simply handing answers to them and then everything fell into place. Quite the contrary. Many times they were at a stalemate with their work, but their desire and perseverance to succeed carried them through. I am quite sure that an open mind played a large role in the next steps forward. When your mind is open it allows the best of your creative and intuitive process to work.

There is a tremendous amount of satisfaction in discovering answers on your own. When you willingly let that be a part of your learning experience you will be far ahead of the crowd who is looking for the "ABC" system. If you choose a mentor, let them guide you, but start out on the right foot. Go in with the attitude that the answers you are looking for are there, however, it is your responsibility to unfold them through your observations and hard work. You can then start to put those answers together to get closer to your goals. You can not realistically expect to trade at the same level of skill as someone who has been trading for a long time. There are a lot of pieces of experience that went into forming, molding, and developing that skill level. That person was willing to travel a road unknown and take each piece and eventually put it in it's proper place. I guarantee you they did not read a book or two and then become a successful trader.

It is also not realistic to expect someone who is not willing to do the work to succeed. To learn a system and instill the proper mindset, it must be an attitude of winning and succeeding from the beginning and of accepting that there will be many unknown bumps and bruises along the way. These bumps and bruises are very necessary to the process, wear them with pride!

Eventually you must step outside the ring of security and put your skill and knowledge to work. This includes resisting the urge to get validation for your actions. To be totally responsible you must be willing to do this. Maybe the novice will have to try a few ideas on their own initiative without validation and be willing to fall and get back up. If you are afraid to fall, and really want someone to hold you up in trading, trading is probably not for you.

The correct mindset from the very beginning can make or break you as a trader.

"Don't be afraid to admit you are wrong: Maladaptive beliefs can be a trader's worst enemy. Many times, one may think, "I can't be wrong on this trade" or "I must capitalize on every opportunity to make a profit." These expectations are so high that they can cause fear and anxiety. When you hold such high expectations for your performance, you place too much pressure on yourself, and cannot maintain a carefree attitude."
Michael S. Shopshire, Ph.D.—
"The Winning Trader, Developing a Mental Edge for Market Success"

The Bradley Stock Market Model

In 1946 Donald Bradley wrote a small paperback book entitled Stock *Market Predictions.* It cost a whopping $4.00 (which in 1947 was a lot of money). Lelewlyn Publications from Minnesota sold very few copies. Bradley only included 2 years of data for the book from 1947-1948. The book was not mass marketed and laid in obscurity for many years.

During the transition years from pattern recognition into astrology (I have returned in earnest) the book was given to me by one of my mentors Dr. Ruth Miller of Indiana. The importance of the little pamphlet would not be revealed to me until 1987. Astrology had pulled me into its intricate web and I was writing Astro Cycles – a Bi-Weekly publication featuring stock indices and commodities. The astrological data I was using came from the Astro Computing Company of San Diego, California. Neil Michelson, the owner, had become a good friend and introduced me to many aspects of astrology that I wasn't even aware they existed. When I mentioned the Bradley book and the sideral graph, Neil volunteered to run the tests to see if it could pass rigid statistical study. Good financial data was not readily available until 1876, ten years after the Civil War. I remember this well because I was only 10 at the time.

Neil proceeded to run all years from 1876 to 1987. The results were amazing! Although it didn't work every year, statistically it was better than 65% predictable at forecasting the trend of the stock market for the year. What is truly incredible is the fact that you can do these trends decades in advance.

Why it works is an elusive answer. It is the reason I came back to pattern recognition. The chart patterns repeat and are predictable within a chaotic market environment. In order to keep it simple I found that the ratios and patterns are what make it tradable and profitable.

The Bradley model has been programmed by our friends at Ensign Software and will now be featured as a weekly segment of the Trading Tutor newsletter.

Those of you in search of answers about what may cause this should read Dr. Al Larsen's classic book, *My Electric Life*. The book describes a theory of electron magnetic energy that sure makes sense. It should be in everyone's library (only $25.00).

"Successful traders thing in terms of probabilities. Rather than looking at the outcome of a single trade by itself, they view it as merely on outcome among a set of outcomes. They believe that overall their trading strategy will give them an edge, and allow them to come out ahead if they make enough trades."

Michael S. Shopshire, Ph.D.—
"The Winning Trader, Developing a Mental Edge for Market Success"

NIKKEI DOW UPDATE

(Written December 2002)

Bad economic reports on the state of Japan are continuing to flow from the major investment houses of Wall Street. These reports outline how really bad it is in Japan now. I would give all of my Xmas presents back to Santa if I could see what they were saying at the top in December 1989.

The news must be bad! That is why their stock market is so low. At major bottoms we should expect negative sentiment at extremely high levels if not at record levels.

Our target on the Nikkei Dow continues to be near the 7800 – 8000 levels. Once this level is reached we will begin our campaign on the bullish side. Rest assured there will be few people willing to step in and buy Japanese stocks. Let's defy human nature – *Trade what you see – Not what you believe.*

"Successful traders take responsibility for their actions. They believe their success is due to their well-developed skills and persistent effort, rather than a matter of circumstance, luck, or chance."
Michael S. Shopshire, Ph.D.—
"The Winning Trader, Developing a Mental Edge for Market Success"

No Expectations – No Opinions

The biggest source of agony and frustration in trading comes from our expectations of what a market should or should not do! Agony becomes intense when we fail to act to correct our original assumption of our market expectations.

THERE IS NO MISTAKE IN BEING WRONG – THE

"You are fully alive and capable of making this day into whatever you want it to be. Though you often cannot control the situations that come along, you always can control the way you deal with them."

Ralph S. Marston, Jr.—The Daily Motivator

NOW

Tomorrow is promised to no one. All we ever have are the few precious moments in the present. We live in the NOW! We may focus on the past and future but we live in the present right now. A single heartbeat separates us from taking the journey beyond death. And an incredible journey it must be because no one has come back to describe it, at least no one with real proof (only exception is Jesus).

Trading in the now moment is very important because we never know what is going to happen next nor do we know if we will win or lose! Trading in the NOW means to prepare for the unexpected. This requires stop-loss orders and an active trading plan geared to protect risk. Spend your time on watching your losses! Losers are results oriented but winners are execution oriented.

Living in the NOW moment allows you to control that which is available today. When you do this you can reverse the letters in NOW and see what you have – WON! The ability to do the things you can do and control the things you can control is the difference between the unsuccessful and successful trader. *"Take care of your losses and your profits will take care of themselves."* - Amos Barr Hostetter

Death escapes no one so it is not to be feared. What should be feared (and avoided at all cost) is living in the past or future. Yesterday is history, tomorrow is a mystery, which leaves us with the present. This must be why most presents are gift-wrapped.

"Whatever your fear, the only way you can overcome it is to meet it head on. Do the thing you fear, and fear will have no control over you."
Ralph S. Marston, Jr.—The Daily Motivator

Overtrading

The best way to stop overtrading is to turn off your monitor after initiating a trade. The monitor is your enemy – not your friend. It will cause you to focus on the upticks if you are long and on the downticks if you are short! The monitor is a mirror of your psychological weaknesses.

Overtrading is the result of improper trade preparation. It's difficult to overtrade when you begin the day fully prepared. Trade what you see – not what you hear during the day. Plan your trades and trade your plan. Prior Planning Prevent Problems – the four "P's" of risk management. Overtrading is the essence of trading frustration. Trying to "catch" a good trade regardless of risk involved. It's the ultimate in trading suicide. Overtrading reduces your probability of success because you are trading without a plan.

"What you do today can improve all your tomorrows. What you do today can change the world. Today is the key. If not today, then when?"
Ralph S. Marston, Jr.—The Daily Motivator

Pack Your Own Parachute

One of our country's elite fighting forces is the United States paratrooper. These soldiers sky dive out of airplanes at incredible heights carrying full battle gear ready to attack behind enemy lines. This preparation is not done overnight! Why would you think that trading preparation would be any different?

Paratroopers spend the early days of their training on the aerodynamics of the parachute and how to get it ready. If you think jumping out of an airplane is easy you should try it sometime. For many traders it would be easier than trying to make money from the markets.

A trader must learn to pack his own trading parachute. It is the lifeline to his continued success and longevity as a trader. The trading parachute is the money management system he employs. Virtually no trading system will work without a sound money management system. It doesn't need to be fancy but it needs to address some key issues:

First – it should consider the "Risk of Ruin", meaning what will happen if everything the trader does, does not work. It's the exact opposite of a best case scenario. When the trader can face the worst and still continue it says something very positive about confidence.

Second – The money management system should describe exactly how much trading capital could be used to place a trade. As a guideline, professional money uses ½ of 1% of available capital as risk on any one trade. This is a maximum percentage usually implemented by short-term hedge funds. Diversified mutual funds will use less capital per trade.

Third - Most traders start out under capitalized. Usually $25,000 will be needed to see if the trader can make a reasonable return at trading. If he risks 2% on each trade ($500) it should keep him in the game. However, if he starts with 8 losing trades his confidence will be shaken somewhat. The key to the process is too keep on trading because we deal in probabilities not certainties. It's probably just as bad for his confidence if he starts with 8 winners. Then his confidence is too high.

Stay balanced and take all the signals for what they really are – the next trade in a series of trades. Trading is a journey not a destination!

“”What have you always wanted? What have you always dreamed of being, doing, or having? Today is your opportunity to go for it. Today is your day to take the first step, to take positive action, to take control of your life and your future. Today is only here once. Use it while you have it. Make it count; make it special as only you can do.”

Ralph S. Marston, Jr.—The Daily Motivator

Pain is the Other Side of Strength

There is an old Chinese adage that says *“that which does not destroy me will make me stronger.”* It refers to the internal battles with one’s self. Trading is certainly an internal battle. Once you conquer the man in the mirror the battle is won. As Socrates said, *“know thyself.”*

Trading can release levels of emotional pain capable of bringing down the best trader. Reports of suicide, although a rare event, are always frightening. I can remember the last days of the great trader Frankie Joe in the mid 80’s. He was one of the best on the street but to himself he was a failure. In his 30’s, he checked out of the game!

Pain is the body’s “red light” system to alert us of a problem. In trading, the source of this pain must be uncovered to prevent it from being fatal.

Most pain in trading comes from these sources:

1. Holding a loss day after day and watching it go lower and lower (reverse if short).
2. Receiving margin calls each day and meeting them to have some hope that the stock will reverse itself.
3. Watching a trade soaring to the sky and you didn't have the courage to buy it.

Trading in pain is a recipe for disaster. This is especially true of neophyte traders who use revenge trading to recoup their losses. Adding to losing positions will be the executioner in these cases. Recent examples of Linux ($320 to $12/share) and Kr. Koop ($70 to $0.70/share) plus hundreds of others amply illustrate this point.

Pain relief is just a phone call away! Do the right thing – exit the position – It does three things for immediate relief:

1. It stops the bleeding in your account and preserves capital.
2. It allows you to think clearly for the first time in a long time.
3. It gives you quiet time to realize what you're doing wrong and develop a trading strategy to recoup your losses.

Trading Hint: If you are in a long or short position and losing and it is past five days and it is getting worse - don't imagine that it's going to get better. You could just as well pour gasoline over yourself and begin smoking! The chances are about equal that you will come out OK!

"Expect the best from life and you'll generally get it."
Ralph S Marston, Jr.—The Daily Motivator

Painting a Picture

Amos Barr Hostetter, founder of commodity Corporation, was a brilliant yet simple man. Easily one of the greatest traders and teachers of any era. Amos was instrumental in the careers of many of the Market Wizards. He worked tirelessly in the profession he loved. When he died in an auto accident in the late 1970's he was taking courses in computer programming, he was 78!

Amos preached a hands-on approach to trading that included hand posting your charts each day. He felt there was a lot to be said for the visual presentation of price bars. They told a story if the trader was willing to listen. Price charts illustrate the amazing geometry of the markets. Price charts are by far the most honest of all indicators because they cannot lie! If prices are going up – there are more buyers, if prices are going down – there are more sellers. Long before the declaration of Bankruptcy by Wcom, Kmart and Enron the prices were collapsing for weeks and months. Insiders were selling all along and they could not hide, prices continued falling.

Moral – ***Trade what you see – Not what you believe.***

Try drawing out you charts by hand and see if you don't develop a better sense for the markets.

"In the words of Thoreau, "For every thousand hacking at the leaves of evil, there is one striking at the root." We can only achieve quantum improvements in our lives as we quit hacking at the leaves of attitude and behavior and get to work on the root, the paradigms from which our attitudes and behaviors flow."
Stephen R. Covey— "The 7 Habits of Highly Effective People"

Pandora's Box

Trading is Pandora's Box. The markets are constantly moving in a way that will trigger our emotions of fear and greed and mirror our inner feelings. This can push traders to both ends of the extremes of fear and greed.

On one end of the extreme is greed, on the other is fear. Our feelings and sentiments about ourselves and perceptions of money all come out and pull at us and can seep into our decision making process with our trades. These decisions can become irrational.

When faced with a trade with accelerating profits, our greed quickly takes hold of us and starts to make decisions for us; it does our thinking for us. How rapidly a 100% profit is not enough. We start to ignore all warning signs that the momentum is starting to subside, we start to focus on every tick and add the money up in our heads, as though it were cash in our pocket. We lose sight that everyone else, with more sense and discipline are leaving the trade or have left the trade. We look up and find ourselves to be the ones left to "turn out the lights". And now the cousin of greed has entered the trade with us - fear. It starts to take hold and push us the other direction. We are no longer self-assured and confident and wealthy, we are now looking at losing face and financial ruin. The fear starts to paralyze our brain. We know intellectually, logically, emotionally we should get out, but it has us. All trading principles are now abandoned. We start praying to the trading gods, "just let it come up one more time, I promise I'll get out". This is a doomed trade unless the trader can come to their senses and get back to an objective view.

I believe most traders have a difficult if not impossible time cutting their losses for two simple reason; fear and greed. People do not like to feel bad, especially in degrees of extreme. We will rationalize and not face the reality rather than admit defeat. Our brains seem to help us by making up all the irrational reasons for staying in a bad trade. Our focus becomes very small and limited.

Try and develop or learn a trading strategy that is suited to your personality. More importantly learn about yourself, learn where your boundaries are. Find ways to stay objective and balanced. Trading while in a mental state of fear or greed will be lethal to your trading career. Some relaxing and breathing techniques may be helpful.

Everyday, thousands upon thousands of traders are opening Pandora's Box and unleashing the demons of fear and greed.

"Breakthroughs refer to new ways of perceiving the world. They occur when you give yourself permission to effectively express you vision. They give you the courage to take action consistent with your commitment to your vision and not in terms of your self-protective needs or your limited notion of who you are."

Ari Kiev— "Trading to Win"

Past, Present and Futures

Yesterday is history. Tomorrow is a mystery. So all we have is the present (and that's why they are gift-wrapped). The best way to prepare for the future is to be thankful for what you have in the present. Focus on what's available today! This is why trading is so incredible! Every thing the trader prepares for each day is applicable to life's little (or big) lessons. The decisions, the failures, the ecstasy and the incredible freedom are what drive the train to success. Each step is a cleansing process that builds confidence and character. And the best part is that they can be passed on to your children and your peers. Nothing helps a child as much as a loving parent who is living their dream! It cannot be faked or disguised because it comes from the heart and soul of the trader. Doing something that you love to do puts you in a perpetual vacation mode. Remember the words of the Chinese seer Confucius, *"The man who works at what he loves is on a permanent vacation."*

You can't get there by worrying about the future or lamenting on the past. Live for today, these 24 hours, 1440 minutes and 86,400 seconds are yours to use as you choose – only you! When they are gone, the are gone forever!

"The market is a force bigger than any one trader. If you go against it, you will feel pain. The traders who go with the tide are more free and easy. They don't like the pain. They like themselves. They know there is no point in fighting the force of the market. They let go of their egos and admit that the market is greater than they are."
Ari Kiev— "Trading to Win"

Putting it on Paper

At one time or another you will experience a large loss in trading, sometimes the large loss can come at one time or it can be cumulative over a period of time. The loss can be due to unexpected market events, a natural string of losses that your method incurred your own trading errors, or a combination of both. At these times it can be difficult for the trader to look at, it can be painful. When these times come along, force yourself to look at the losses, don't put your head in the sand and ignore your statements or not record the losses as if not recording them means they didn't happen.

Decide that you will always act professionally and write the losses down. This in itself can be the start to getting back on the right track. By looking at each trade you will clearly be able to see which category the losses fall into. If they are due to unexpected market events, dust yourself off and realize those times will happen and go on. If they are due to a natural string of losses your method is going through, same thing. If they are due to your own errors then look at those errors and see where you got off track. Make notes of how you can get back on track. Have some forgiveness of yourself and then get back on track.

To hide in the sand is a big mistake, it is not facing reality and it is not being responsible. You must learn to face reality everyday in the markets and nothing is more real than your personal profit and loss statement.

"Be willing to live daily in the gap between where you are now and where you wish to be. The simple decision to act will reduce any fear or self-doubt you may have and will activate motivational processes within you. From the decision to take action you set in motion a positive self-fulfilling prophecy. Each day, begin to do what is necessary to realize that goal."
Ari Kiev— "Trading to Win"

REACTING TO NEWS

(Written Early March, 2003)

If there is one truth in the market it is probably the fact that news follows the trend. Bullish news brings higher prices, bearish news brings lower prices. Think back to 1999 when the NASDAQ was flying. Analysts would upgrade earnings of the typical *pizza.com* and the stock would open higher by 20% or more. A classic mania was in place but few market participants were even born to remember that history does repeat itself.

The current situation with Iraq is a case in point. Reporters constantly bombard us with news regarding the upcoming war with Iraq. Oil prices have dropped $7.00/barrel since the completion of the butterfly top pattern a few short weeks ago. War with Iraq is far from a certainty. Beware of news reports of any kind. Let the price chart dictate the direction of the market. *"Markets are seldom wrong – men often are"* – Roy Longstreet.

Market participants cannot hide their involvement. If prices are moving higher – the buyers are in control and if the prices are moving lower – the sellers are in control.

Past favorites such as Enron, Worldcom, Kmart and CMGI were heading down long before most of the bad news was reported. News leaks out long before the reporters get the information. To prevent a disaster in trading stocks or futures a simple order is available to everyone. It is called a stop-loss order. The name tells it all! You are stopping the loss from getting bigger. Your first loss is always you smallest. Should you delay in executing your order the loss usually increases and most probably exponentially. Learn to use stop loss orders and learn to use them religiously, fanatically, and **UNEMOTIONALLY.**

"All successful traders have a defined, written trading plan...A trader who does not consistently abide by his or her trading plan is doomed to failure. Why have a plan and not follow it? Each guideline and rule must be included with reason and purpose. All successful traders and investors consistently follow their trading plan and know that if they violate their trading plan it will always be costly in the long run."

Robert Miner— "Dynamic Trading"

Respect for Margin

One of the cardinal rules of in the business of trading is the proper use of margin requirements which are set by the exchanges to protect its customers. This protection comes in two forms, the initial margin and the maintenance margin. Initial margin is what you need to open a position. Maintenance margin comes into play when the trade begins to go against you (heaven forbid).

This cardinal rule of margin is quite simple – Never, ever answer a margin call! Never, never, never! A margin call is one of the most informative things in all of trading. First it tells you that your analysis is completely wrong (admit that first of all). Second, the margin call is telling you that you are undercapitalized. Third and most importantly – you are trading without a stop which also means that you are trading without a trading plan. Do yourself a huge favor – close the position and do something else for a living. Trading isn't for you. If you can't play by the rules – don't play the game!

"What I find among those I teach is, one, they want to be right.
Two, they don't want to take a loss."
Walter Bressert— "When Super Traders Meet Kryptonite"

Responsibility

Trading requires the ultimate trait of responsibility because the markets are like a river and we have to jump in to be involved. Once in we are in the grasp of the market and all of its forces, you alone can save yourself!

Once you are in the market you have the ultimate responsibility – no one else! You place the orders and you take the profits, you alone take the loss or exit the trade prematurely or stay in the trade too long.

Don't fall into the habit of making excuses on why something went wrong! I have heard them all a hundred times or more. *"Forget your profits, but forget your losses faster."* – Amos Barr Hostetter

Taking responsibility can be improved by including a few steps or reminders in your trading plan. What works for one trader might not work for another. One step I take to handle this is to place a written statement on my computer (it is the only written statement on my computer). The statement says;

1. Has the pattern changed from the original pattern?
2. Has the initial price objective been reached?

If the answer to both of these questions is yes then you can exit the trade. However, if the answer is no then the trade must continue because trading is a business of dealing with probabilities, not certainties. We never, ever know which trades will work. The problem arises when we only "think" we know! I learned this strategy form Amos Bar Hostetter during his years at Commodity Corporation.

"It's when you're not happy that you can discover that what's between you and that next level is you."
Adrienne Toghraie

Risk

John Hill, my mentor and life long friend gave me a banner with the words – *"He who knows not what he risks – Risks all!"* Unless you know the exact amount you are risking in a trade you are risking financial chaos. Knowing when to get out is more important than knowing when to get in. Traders must learn to not stay at the party for too long. It's much better to be out of a market wishing you were in, than being in a market wishing you were out!

Risk is the only variable the trader can control. He never knows which trades will work. He can never know how much profit will be available (if any) in a trade. But he can control his risk on each and every trade.

If there is one common thread among great traders it is their aversion to risk. You must have capital to play in the game and there should never be a trade where you are willing to risk it all. Never go for broke – you just might get it!

"The difference between winning and losing, success and failure depends on just a few simple but profound choices, Ironically, knowledge alone will not provide the solution. It is not enough to know what to do. You must consistently do what you know."

Robert Koppel and Howard Abell—
"The Inner Game of Trading"

RISKING

Trading is all about risk control! The following excerpt is from one of my favorite audiotapes, 'Risking' by David Viscount. I keep this on my desk to remind me each day to keep "risking." Only a person who risks is truly free.

To laugh is to risk appearing the fool.
To weep is to risk appearing sentimental.
To expose feelings is to risk exposing your true self.
To place your ideas, your dreams, before a crowd is to risk their loss.
To live is to risk dying. To hope is to risk despair. To try is to risk failure.
But risks must be taken, because the greatest hazard in life is to risk nothing.
The person, who risks nothing, does nothing, has nothing, and is nothing.
They may avoid suffering and sorrow, but they cannot learn, feel, change, grow, love...live.
Only a person who risks is free.

—Dr. David Viscount

"As we have clearly seen, it is the innergame of the trader that determines if the system or the specific analytical methods of choice will be successful."
Robert Koppel and Howard Abell—
"The Inner Game of Trading"

Rockets Red Glare!

There are rare events in the stock market that leave a huge trail of unanswered questions. October 19, 1987 was one such event – volume 600 million shares, only 8 issues on the NYSE were up that day (out of 3300 issues). A panic by anyone's definition. Later we were to find out that the Federal Reserve Board opened their vaults and let Wall Street know that "It stops going down today". The massive influx of capital and the subsequent rally had marked the most significant bottom since 1982. Ironically the low of the Dow Jones on October 19, 1987 (1600+) was an exact .618 (Fibonacci retracement) of the August 1982 low.

On September 21, 2000, Intel surprised "the street" by issuing an earnings warning. The stock closed on Wednesday night at $61/share. Reaction to the news in after market trading was devastating. Intel dropped to $48 – down 13 points in a few seconds. This was a $100 billion loss in capital.

At the end of trading on Friday September 22nd, 2000 the NASDAQ market sent a signal to the world – a Rockets Red

Glare! Intel had traded 304 million shares in a single day surpassing the old record of 187 million shares held by Oracle in 1997.

Here is some food for thought:

1. Intel's volume was ½ of the total volume on the NYSE on Black Friday – October 19, 1997.
2. Normal volume for Intel is 38 million shares vs. 304 million on September 22nd.
3. Intel opened on the low of the day at 46 and a fraction and stayed in a 2 point trading range the entire day (46 ½ - 48 ½).
4. The above observation is technically the most amazing accomplishment in my opinion. 304 million shares changing hands in a stock that just lost 100 billion of its capitalization and it was done in a two-point range. For every buyer there must be a seller and they were there in droves on Sept. 22nd.
5. The average trading range of Intel is approximately 5 points a day!
6. The initial response to the Intel earnings warning pushed stocks lower across the NYSE, NASDAQ and S&P 500. However, by mid day many shares had rallied to be up on the day. Only the chipmakers were unable to rally.
7. Triple digit losses were seen in the DOW and NASDAQ. The DOW JONES made a miracle recovery and ended up over 80 points for the day; and it did this while one of its key components (Intel) was down 13 points or 20%!

How can we interpret all of this activity? Out of chaos comes change! It is this writer's opinion that Intel is at the edge of a cliff. It can either sail off into oblivion or step back and re-group. Keep in mind that during the 1920's and 30's the United States had over 2000 car companies – today we have 2 ½!

Intel's September 22nd low occurred at an exact Fibonacci expansion (1.27) from the previous high. Intel should hold the $46/share level to remain bullish. Going below $45/share would make this trader very nervous. This is one of the lowest risk opportunities that Intel has presented to the market in many years.

In Chinese writings the characters for risk and opportunity are the same. The use in the sentence determines the meaning. It is the same for Intel's stock now!

"The reason a lot of people do not recognize opportunity is because it usually goes aound wearing overalls looking like hard work."
Thomas A. Edison

Routines

Developing routines can be very helpful for your trading. Every trader has a little different routine that they are in the habit of doing. Some things that can be part of a trading regiment include some things outside of trading such as; eating a healthy diet, getting regular exercise, making sure you get enough sleep and setting aside time for social activities outside of trading and taking time off when necessary.

A trading routine should of course always include ample time for preparation for the next days trading. Deciding which markets you will be looking at for a potential trade, preparing a trade plan for those markets should become routine. Another important area that can be included in your trading routines is taking time to set the proper mind set for the days trading. This can be making sure you have plenty of time before the markets open and double checking your preparations from the night before, having something healthy to eat for energy, reading a few pages of something inspirational can certainly help put the trader in the proper frame of mind.

Whatever you develop as a routine will become your personal signature of your trading style and will help to keep you in a consistent mode for your trading.

""So much left undone."
Michelangelo Buonarroti—(1475-1564)

Running Scared

"Running Scared" is an expression we use to denote uncertainty in a particular trading situation. By definition, it means trading just a little in excess of one's stress point. Quite often I have used the expression, "I'm running scared – and enjoying it." I've come to realize that often it is during those times when I'm scared that I am happiest. While at first glance this may sound contradictory, it can be explained. True happiness does not come from doing an easy job. It comes with the afterglow of satisfaction which follows the achievement of a difficult job that demands our very best. Running scared permits one to behold the power of faith to work miracles as expressed in these inspiring words: *"Fear knocked at the door, Faith opened it - and lo, there was no one there."*

When one is scared (but not frightened, there's a big difference), he is stimulated to think. Quite often this is the only condition conducive to productive thought. Man is a lazy creature. We all tend to be as lazy as we dare to be. So long as affairs are running smoothly, there is a tendency to take things for granted. We assume that the market is on course, that there is no need for concern, that there is no risk in this "best of all possible worlds."

But in the real world in which we live, change is the only thing certain.

Change has a habit of rudely awakening lethargic or complacent traders. Unless we sometimes find ourselves running scared, it is almost a certainty that we are not living up to our real potential. There are far worse things than occasionally running scared. The worst possible fate is to simply vegetate – to live so far under our stress point that we are never forced to think.

Running scared gives one a chance to flood the dark corners of fear and superstion with the bright light of reason and knowledge, overcoming fancy with fact, dispensing hobgoblins of the imagination and revealing the truth that is basic to our way of life.

The Chinese use the same symbol for danger and for opportunity. The truth of this seeming paradox has been brought forcefully home to me many times in trading. It is best illustrated by a statement from a successful young trader: "I knew we would not make any money on that trade. We never did run scared on it."

"Diamonds are polished by grit, men by adversity."

"If you find a path with no obstacles, it probably doesn't lead anywhere."
Reverend Sunnan Kubose

Science vs. Art

Trading has been described as a mixture of science and art sprinkled with ample portions of intuition. This is probably as good a description as you might ever find. There are no formal schools that give educational degrees in trading; however I would expect this to change in the next few years. Several of the more prominent MBA programs have included formal classes on some elements of trading, but it is hardly a complete coverage of the essentials of trading. Traders search for their own knowledge through the use of books, mentors, seminars and the internet.

Financial publications such as Business Week, Forbes and Fortune are including more articles on the subject of trading. Many times however, these articles focus on the trading abuses such as the Enron fiasco!

The scientific part of trading is probably the easiest to acquire because it can be reduced to rules and numbers. But trading is far more than numbers and rules! Because trading keeps score by using the root of all evil – money, all of the various aunts and uncles of the emotions family come into the trading equation. At this point in the traders career (a fork in the road) he will be pulled like a giant magnet into the journey of self discovery. Remember the monitor you watch to find your trading signals is in actuality a mirror of yourself. Any psychological flaws seen in the mirror will be reflected in the decisions you base on what you see in the monitor.

There is no better way to improve the art of trading than reading Mark Douglas' book *Trading in the Zone*. This book tears right to the heart of the trader's emotions. After reading *Trading in the Zone* completely it would be of great help to read 4 to 5 pages per day. In this fashion you will have read the book several times each year and each of its informative sentences and phrases will be impaired in your trading psyche forever.

"Let the market make the decisions, not your ego."
Edward Allen Toppel— "ZEN In the Markets: Confessions of a Samurai Trader"

SHORT CUTS

The path of least resistance will usually turn out to be the most arduous. This is also true in trading. Short cuts are usually just that, very short and the cuts can be mighty deep and the bleeding can be difficult to stop. It's always amazed me how the investing public will be led into risky ventures, and they continue to do it even after they know it's not for them!

This business of speculator is a very noble profession but there are few places to learn it from the ground up. One of my closest friends is a very successful trader. Jim Twentyman has been my trading buddy since the early trading days at Conte Commodity and Commodity Corporation. His favorite quote is a true classic. *"Defy human nature and do the work yourself."* Remember it's what you learn after you think you know it all that is really important to you.

Trading is one business where short cuts can be lethal. Examine yourself for what you really want to get out of trading and spend some time on a plan to achieve your goals. If you don't have a plan and a goal it will be impossible for you to know that you've arrived at your goal!

"Where there is no such thing as no such thing."
Slogan at the Chicago Mercantile Exchange

Signs of Depression

Trading demands preparation, concentration and executions. If your trading is getting worse or making no progress it could be a sign of mild depression. Some of the signs of mild depression are:

- Insomnia
- Lack of appetite
- Not wanting to do anything
- Not showering, shaving or getting dressed in the morning
- Feelings of inadequacies
- Not wanting to talk to friends
- Consumption of alcohol above normal amount
- Spontaneous crying
- Need to be left alone
- Not wanting to talk on the telephone when it rings

This is just a partial list. Should the symptoms become extreme please see a physician, there are excellent medications that can jolt you out of this condition. In addition there are some homeopathic remedies that just might do the trick.

1) Take a three to five day break and do not watch the monitor or the charts at any time.
2) Begin an exercise program –this increases the production of endorphins in our brain, which help raise our spirits.
3) Find a hobby to take your mind off your woes.
4) Begin a positive thinking program into your daily routine – such as Tony Robbins – Personal Power Program.
5) Do something to help someone much more challenged than you. Battered wives and battered children, the homeless, blind elderly people, etc.
6) Change your diet to eat only wholesome foods with no additives. No soft drinks, alcohol, high sugar deserts. Flood your body with water, fresh fruits and vegetables and small amounts of protein.

You do not need to devote a lot of time to any of these but a little of each one will yield recognizable results. If the condition gets worse see your physician!

"What is intuition? You often hear traders say "I am buying or selling this stock on my intuition." The best definition I can give of intuition is that it is instantaneous reasoning. It is something which tells us when we are right or wrong before we have time to reason in out. The way to benefit through intuition is to act immediately, and not stop to reason or ask why. That is what a good tape reader does."

William D. Gann— "Truth of the Stock Tape," 1923

Small Dose – Big Damage

The University of Amsterdam and Leiden University have recently published a research study documenting the effect of small dosages of alcohol while working at a computer monitor designed to find targets on the screen. Does this sound familiar? Subjects given 2 oz of Vodka in orange juice (screwdriver) scored 4 times as many errors as the placebo group. Brain wave measurements were quickly affected via the cerebral cortex. Eight hours after the test researchers administered the same test without the Vodka and although there was some improvement in the errors, the non-alcohol group did significantly better after eight hours. This is further evidence of what my own empirical studies have shown. If I drink wine (and that is the only alcohol I use) during the trading week it affects my trading. Knowledge of this has kept my consumption of champagne or merlot limited to Friday and Saturday. Occasionally I will have a glass mid-week but it is not often and is one glass.

Alcohol destroys the brain cells in all traders. We need every edge we can get. If you are drinking during the trading week you are not at your peak performance. Should you be drinking during market hours you need to get into a twelve-step program immediately.

"One great mistake the man makes who watches the ticker all the time is that he trades too often."
William D. Gann— "Truth of the Stock Tape,"
1923

So You Want to Pick a Top (or Bottom)?

There is nothing more illusive (and also satisfying) as placing a trade at the exact low or high of a move. It's as if some magical wizard will highlight your equity run with an asterisk, announcing to the world, "that you did pick that exact spot." There ought to be a bonus prize for the few traders who actually do this, but alas there is none.

From the minds of two of the greatest trader's who ever lived comes some savvy information on the subject. Amos Barr Hostetter, one of the founders of Commodity Corporation, used to remark that once you've picked that exact point where the market will turn, just add another 30% to the move and wait. This is sound advice.

In the past two decades few traders have experienced the success of Paul Tudor Jones! Mr. Jones exploits in the markets have reached the legendary status they deserve. My favorite tidbit is from an article in the Wall Street Journal when he was interviewed on his trading. The reporter was very excited by P.T.J.'s recent success in the Treasury bond market. What follows is a paraphrase of that interview. The reporter said to P.T.J. that he must have been elated that he picked the exact low day to buy T-bonds before they exploded to the upside! Mr. Jones replied that the statement was only partially correct. He said a more accurate statement would be: "Paul Tudor Jones correctly forecast the recent low in Treasury Bonds – after failing to forecast the low on his last five attempts!" You can rest assured that P.T.J. had a firm grip on the risk assessment on ***all*** of those trades. His approach to risk control is what makes him a great trader ("a market wizard").

So you still want to pick a top or bottom? If so then you must define what you are willing to risk! One of the ways to do this is to find a pattern that appears at tops and bottoms. Presented in this article is the Butterfly Pattern that was the discovery of Bryce Gilmore (developer of the Waver Trader) and me. We found this pattern in the wee small hours of an extended research session.

If you take some time to study these two examples you will see the beautiful harmony in the pattern. Not only is an AB=CD in the final impulse wave but the expansion wave is 1.27 (1.27 is the square root of 1.618). This is the proverbial moment of truth and the outcome will be known almost immediately. Protective stops should be placed just above the expansion wave. Usually 2% of trading equity is the maximum risk exposure. When these patterns work, the result is quite rewarding. Unfortunately, probabilities are in force and "butterfly's" only some of the time!

"People underestimate the time it takes to succeed as a trader. Some people come here and think they can sit with me for a week and become great traders. How many people when they went to college would've thought to walk up to the professor and say, 'I know the course is for a semester, but I think a week should be enough for me to get it.' Gaining proficiency is the same in trading as in any other profession—it requires experience and experience takes time."

Mark D. Cook—Interview in "Stock Market Wizards," by Jack Schwager

Some Things never Change

Few of us would argue that three of the most important discoveries of the last 150 years have been electricity, automobiles and computers. All of us depend heavily on their availability. But it was only the early pioneers of these industries that were able to amass great wealth.

One of my favorite books that I've accumulated over the past five decades is a little paperback published in the late 1930's and written by F.L. Allen. The book, *Only Yesterday*, is a masterpiece that chronicles the events leading up to the great bull market of the 1920's and the depression that followed. So many historical facts are illustrated throughout the text.

One of my personal favorites concerns the automobile industry. At the height of the roaring twenties there were over 2000 automobile companies in the United States alone. Five decades later there were only three. The lesson here is very important – you must get in early and don't forget that trends and business conditions can change quickly and frequently do!

It was in reading the history of financial boom and bust cycles that led me to the pattern recognition and swing trading methodology I use today. Trade what you see – Not what you believe!

A testament to how things change becomes apparent when you look at what happened to these six famous people of the roaring twenties. Maybe you can see some similarities to today's times!

1. The president of the largest steel company, Charles Schwab, died a pauper.
2. The president of the largest Gas Company, Edward Hopson, went insane.
3. The president of the New York Stock Exchange, Richard Whitney, was released from prison to die at home.
4. The greatest wheat speculator, Arthur Cooger, died abroad penniless.
5. The president of the Bank of International Settlement shot himself.
6. The Great Bear of Wall Street, Jesse Livermore, committed suicide. (He did *not* die penniless, as is the popular theory.)

"Profits make traders feel powerful and give them an emotional high. They try to get high again, put on reckless trades, and give back their profits... The few survivors realize that the main trouble is not with their methods, the trouble is with their thinking. They can change and become successful traders."

Dr. Alexander Elder— "Trading for a Living"

Some Thoughts on Investment Strategy

(Written on the first anniversary of September 11)

One of the most widely followed theories on investment strategies is that of the buy and hold philosophy. It is usually accompanied by its sister strategy of averaging down stock prices. Let's take a look at how these might have worked on the following stocks – Worldcom, Enron, Global Crossing, K-Mart, Lucent, CMGI, Ericsson, Juniper Networks, Sycamore Networks and a great many others.

Keep in mind that during the great bear market of 1929 – 1932 only half of the Dow Jones stocks were able to avoid bankruptcy. The point of this exercise is to remember that the charts do not lie to you. If prices are dropping there are more sellers. If prices are rising there are more buyers. In my forty years of trading, I think I only received one stock tip that worked and it was only short term. No, I did not buy the stock.

Examine the stock of Ford Motors. This stock has violated all support points and appears headed toward $5.00/share or insolvency. In 1982 the government bailed out Chrysler after the stock went below $5/share. It was the armored tank division that the government wanted to save. Lee Iacoca knew this and played his card well enough to make a fortune and save the company.

Isn't it ironic that if Ford hits $5/share it will be at the same price it was when it was issued in 1931! Remember the pattern in AOL when it broke $18/share, it looks very similar to Ford.

Stocks continue to retreat from the September 11th emotional high. Stocks opened sharply higher that day as the market breathed a sigh of relief that there was no terrorist activity only to end sharply lower on the day.

""The market does not know you exist. You can do nothing to influence it. You can only control your behavior."
Dr. Alexander Elder— "Trading for a Living"

STAY FOCUSED

Staying focused during the trading day takes patience and practice! It's not about staring at the monitor all day long. That is the ultimate in futility. Do other things while you trade! The markets don't care what position you have in the market. Neophyte traders have a tendency to want to focus on the intraday price swings. Each uptick and downtick brings near draconian reaction. Focus on what needs to be done and just do it. Trading is simple – but it ain't easy!

Take breaks during the trading day. Place your orders and enjoy the day. Your trading plan should cover any contingencies that may occur. The numbers of times that unforeseen events hit the market are quite rare and prices usually proceed where they were going anyway.

A daily regimen or routing can help you stay focused. Habits are like steel cables – you weave a strand a day until they

"At any rate, this catastrophe should teach every-body a lesson. You can't play on the big board without getting a lot of splinters."
Eddie Cantor, Comedian— "Caught Short! A Saga of Wailing Wall Street", 1929

That Uneasy Feeling

Did you ever have the uneasy feeling the so called experts are really *not* experts? You are not alone! In a small oak bookcase that sits on my desk is a collection of books I use frequently. One of the books is titled, *The Experts Speak.* It is a 400 plus compilation of statements made by very famous people and how wrong they really can be. The authors are Chris Cerf and Victor Navasky. Here are some of my favorites:

Stocks – "*Stocks have reached what looks like a permanently high plateau."* Irving Fisher, Yale University, October 1929.

The ultimate timing quote – *"We will not go to war with Japan in 48 hours, 48 days, 48 years."* Wendall Wilke – Republican candidate for President at a breakfast meeting December 7, 1941.

Music – *"We don't like their sound. Groups of guitars are on the way out."* CEO of Decca Records speaking about the Beattles in 1962.

Politics – *"Bill Clinton will lose to any Republican who doesn't drool on stage."* Wall Street Journal editorial, 1995.

Sports – (This quote is very special to me because it features a picture of two of my friends and former students; Jack O'Callahan and Jack Hughes). *"We have two chances to beat the Russians – Slim and None."* Herb Brooks – Coach of U.S. Olympic Hockey team immediately before the U.S. team won the gold Medal in 1980.

There is a point to all of this. There are experts out there but they can be just as wrong as anyone else. This includes this writer. There is one thing that is none negotiable – patterns repeat and they are somewhat predictable!

"Veni, vidi, vici
I came, I saw, I conquered
"Have no fear of perfection, you'll never reach it."
Salvador Dali—1904-1989

The Ancestry of Every Action is Thought

Ralph Waldo Emerson is one of our most beloved literary geniuses. This statement is a powerful reminder of the vastness of the human mind.

Each thought carries an idea. Each idea carries a goal. Each goal contains a destiny. If you change your destiny, you change your life.

Habits are thoughts that have become attached to our psyche. Habits are like strong steel cables and you weave a strand each day until the habit becomes almost unbreakable. The trick is make your habits positively charged.

Scientists universally agree that the power of the human brain far exceeds any computer ever built. Our brain uses about 7% of its total capacity. Whenever I read an article or watch a program focusing on those rare individuals known as "Savants" I am amazed. These super geniuses exhibit almost god-like qualities in the use of their brains. Unfortunately, they don't develop to what we consider normal behavioral humans. Many can only do one thing! Remember Raymond Babbitt, "The Rain Man"! He could sure count cards while playing black jack.

Thoughts should be positive at all times! Work on removing negative thoughts. Ask yourself where the negative thought originated. Cut it out at its roots and replace it with a seedling of positive thoughts. Your forest will grow strong with positive seedlings.

"Life is hardly more than a fraction of a second.
Such a little time to prepare
oneself for eternity."
Paul Gauguin—French Painter

The Economics of War

(Written early 2003)

Every day over the past several months the financial press has bombarded the public with how bearish the advent of the war with Iraq will be on the
U.S. economy.

This is especially true for the reporters at CNBC. It appears to be an obsession with this program. Guest after guest is called into the debate on the coming war. The past week a Saudi prince was quoted as saying that $100/barrel oil sounded about right. He could hardly be accused of having a conflict of interest could he?

Wouldn't it be refreshing for the reporters to have a market statistician on their program? Wars may have a short-term bearish affect on the economy but the history of the stock market shortly following the outbreak of war is very bullish over the past 150 years. This takes us back to the Civil War!

The news follows the stock market. Simply stated it means that the stock market traditionally has already discounted most impending disasters including wars and threats of war.

In contrast to the invasion into Kuwait by Iraq in 1990, this war may be provoked by another party. There are so many variables in the pot that anything could happen. The market is still reeling from the World Trade Center attack of Sept. 11 last year. Any external shock could jolt the market at any time. But the key think to keep in mind is that it will most likely be a buying opportunity for 2 reasons:

First – War is bullish on the stock market – History has indicated this bias.
Second – The stock markets around the world have been in bear markets for over 2 years and are in very over-sold condition.

Does this guarantee that prices will rise in stocks with the start of war? Of course not, because nothing is guaranteed in our business. We are opportunists and try to find price patterns that present these opportunities to us.

"One can have no smaller or greater mastery than mastery of oneself."
Leonardo da Vinci

The Good Call

One of my personal pet peeves in trading is the one known as the "good call". It is when a trader "calls" the market direction on a trade and is then applauded by other traders. Shouting or calling out a trade is done by almost all market participants at one time or another during their market careers.

What is futile about the process is that it means absolutely nothing. It's an exercise in ego enhancement. A good trader should be applauded for exiting a bad position quickly rather "calling" what a market should or should not do!

Remember that losers are results oriented and winners are execution oriented. These are two entirely different processes and the professional trader who focuses on risk management at all times knows this!

So whenever one of those rare events happens and I happen to get lucky on market direction, just laugh and forget it because the next one may be a loser.

You must learn to fish for yourself anyway. Never, ever expand on the fishing skills of others to feed your P&L statement.

"If people knew how hard I worked to get my mastery, it wouldn't seem so wonderful at all."
Michelangelo Buonarroti—
(1474-1564)

The Island Principle

Ancient explores had a cardinal rule when they were about to explore new territory, especially islands. If you are going to an island, you better take everything you need because you won't be able to find it once you are on the island.

Trading is a lot like being on an island. We must have everything we need before we start. Unfortunately, there are few traders who ever start with all the necessities. Most of what they really need they build during the process. Think of how different your trading experience would have been if you started out with a sound foundation of trading principles.

If you're sailing toward the trading island here are essentials you might want to bring;

First – a sound money management philosophy.

Second – a true understanding of your trading plan including why it doesn't work all the time.

Third – this is the least of the necessary essentials, starting capital. Make sure that the starting capital is reasonable but also disposable income that you can afford to lose. Once trading is learned, capital becomes less of an issue because the trader understands the dimensions of risk and controls his trading as it relates to risk.

Risk is the only thing we can control in the risk/reward equation. Probability on a trade is never 100% and the profit amount is never known. Control your risk and the trading island you land on will be fun and maybe even ecstatic.

"Making money is art and working is art and good business is the best art."
Andy Warhol

The Mental Challenge

Some things in the business of trading or speculation are non-negotiable. I can say with 110% confidence that the mental part of trading is the most important. Much like the great New York Yankee catcher Lawrence "Yogi" Berra has stated, *"Hitting is 90% mental and the other 50% is technique!"*

It's not *what* you think – it's *how* you think. Trading is more like sports competition than most traders realize. Professional athletes have a set routine for pre-game conditioning that is an automatic response. It's their way of "anchoring" their behavior to get the same response regardless of the circumstances or distractions.

In the mid 1980's I was fortunate to have Mark Douglas, author of *The Disciplined Trader* and *Trading in the Zone* come into my life! We were in Las Vegas speaking at a trade show. I wanted to hear Mark speak but he insisted that I spend 4 hours at a John Bradshaw seminar going on at the same hotel but a totally non-trading venue. I grudgingly took his advice after he assured me that the population (about 100) in the Bradshaw seminar was identical in psychological make-up as the trading population.

John Bradshaw is a trained psychologist and the author of many books on coping with life's problems. In those four hours I heard bone chilling stories of parental abuse, child abuse, sexual abuse, physical abuse and just about everything with the exception of outright murder. If indeed any of these people were in the stock market (as most were middle to upper middle class) it would be very difficult for them to be successful. All of us carry some "baggage" around with us all the time. Trading requires that you check your bags each trading day. Knowledge that the baggage exists is the first step in controlling its side effects.

I realized how important the mental aspect of our business is in those four hours. Although I did not suffer from the incredibly vivid cruelties, I did realize that there were some things I needed to address. In my case, it was the relationship, a very stormy one that I had with my father. After reconciling this part of my past I could finally trade without guilt. My dad thought what I did was pure gambling and it hurt a lot of people. My first full year of trading I made more than my dad had made in 20 years! I believe that he resented this and went to his grave without speaking to me in his last two years.

"The game of speculation is the most uniformly fascinating game in the world. But it is not a game for the stupid, the mentally lazy, the man of inferior emotional balance, nor for the get-rich-quick adventurer. They will die poor."
Jesse L. Livermore— "How to Trade In Stocks"

The Nature of Gaps

Price gaps occur on nearly all charts at some time. These gaps are filled eventually, some take days others weeks or months. A price gap is the result of a change in the continuity of thought in the investment arena. Currency devaluations, climate changes, or political upheavals are some of the more common causes of price gaps. The size of the price gap and when it occurs in the trend can be an important indication as to whether the price gap is an exhaustion gap or a breakaway gap.

Exhaustion gaps are near the ends of extensive price moves. These are trends that are well established and have been trending for weeks or months. At these times the financial prcss is constantly bombarding the public about the current fundamental conditions in the market. Remember this: "The news always follows the trend." Prices are where they are for a reason – to match buyers and sellers! Exhaustion gaps are filled quickly and serve no other purpose than to entrap the final entrants into a market (either long or short).

Breakaway gaps are the most powerful! They also last far longer than exhaustion gaps. When a market suddenly gaps on a chart you can assume one thing – someone who knows something is willing to enter the market regardless of price. Stock earnings, legal decisions, FDA announcements occur in stocks on a regular basis and affect prices in proportion to the implication of the announcement.

Trading gaps should hold a special amount of respect for the trader because of the risk implications. As a safety measure the trader should wait one or two days before entering. Profit taking is always present in the market so watching intraday price action for several days after the gap will often lead to a low risk entry into the market.

The true reasons for the gap will usually come to light over time. Price charts expose all buyers and sellers, they can not hide. If prices are going up there are more buyers if prices are going down there are more sellers.

"Trading is simple but it ain't easy." – Mark Douglas, *Trading in the Zone*

"There is always the temptation in the stock market, after a period of success, to become careless or excessively ambitious. Then it requires sound common sense and clear thinking to keep what you have. But it is not necessary to lose your money, once you have acquired it, if you will hold fast to sound principles."
Jesse L. Livermore— "How to Trade in Stocks"

The News Follows the Trend

One of the very best market indicators is the reaction to news! The trend of the market follows the news. When the trend stops following the news the technical trader should pay attention. When very bullish news fails to make the market go higher then there is only one direction for the market to move – that direction is down. The same is true for bearish news, except that the market moves higher.

December 19th, 2002 is a good example of this phenomenon referred to as "reaction to the news". The price of gold has been rising steadily over the past several months! Last night the spot price of gold rose as much as $15/oz in Asia, Australia, Hong Kong and Europe! The Financial press had a field day reporting on the soaring gold price. It was the featured story. All of the gold stocks listed in New York were due to open sharply higher, and why wouldn't they! Shortly before the opening of the NYSE, the price of gold was still $7/oz higher on the day. Opening indicators for the gold stocks were sharply higher. However, the opening bell saw the gold stocks open lower, not higher. When all the good news is in the market, that market should not move higher. And it is really major news when the market does not go higher! The lesson to be learned here is to respect what the market is trying to tell you! Markets are seldom wrong -—men often are! Will this be a major top in gold? God only knows and she ain't talking. The signs are there – bearish patterns, major divergences among some of the gold stocks, bullish enthusiasm at record levels, and finally poor reaction to the news! This is a real chance to learn how a market reacts to news. We will do a follow up in a few weeks to see how it unfolded.

"Many years of my life had been devoted to speculation before it dawned upon me that nothing new was happening in the stock market, that price movements were simply being repeated, that while there was variation in different stocks the general price pattern was the same."
Jesse L. Livermore— "How to Trade in Stocks"

The Non Random Nature of Stocks

Recently, there has been one giant step forward for those of us that have believed in the value of technical analysis over the years. An article from academia has verified what we have believed all along – there are non-random patterns in stocks and the stock markets. The article was written by the Ph.D.'s from MIT under the guidance of Andrew Lo. It verified that the typical chart patterns such as *head and shoulders* and *pennants* are in fact repetitive and predictable of future price movement. Welcome to the club!

At the heart of all technical analysis are two of the greatest Scientists/investors who ever walked the earth—Issac Newton and Leonardo Da Vinci.

From Newton, technical analysis gets the law "for every action there is an equal but opposite reaction." This is the backbone of the AB = CD parallel movement pattern presented by H. M. Gartley in 1938. Da Vinci's book on the Fibonacci Summation series presented in his "Codex" notebook illustrates the ever-present nature of these numbers throughout our universe.

OK, so how does this help me in trading? It may not help your trading at all but it points the way to the unchallenged statement that the overall nature of stocks and stock markets are chaotic but within this chaos are non-random patterns that repeat over and over again. If you can find a pattern that repeats and know that it is going to work 2/3 (66%) of the time, then you have powerful information to use because the market is no longer a 50-50 coin toss at this point.

One thing is tantamount in trading whether you use technical analysis, pattern recognition or any of the plethoras of other methods. No one can ever know what the markets are going to do next. No one can ever know how much money is going to be made on the next trade. So the only thing that the trader/investor can control is the amount of risk on the trade. Great traders focus on the amount of money at risk at all times! Winners think, “How much can I lose?” Losers think, “How much can I win?” I suppose this is the reason that all casinos have giant flashing signs showing the jackpots!

"Each time you'll take the step that you're sure you can't, you'll discover that the "you" who would not was only a thought that believed it could not."
Guy Finley— "The Key of the Kings"

The Ten Commandments of Day Trading

It is imperative when day trading to accomplish these important tasks:

First – Conscientious preparation for the day's trading is essential, including knowing projected highs and lows; monitoring market action after economic reports occurring during market hours; and monitoring the effects of the overnight news from around the world. If you trade Foreign Currencies you *must* have access to the Forex overnight markets. The price swings in the 24-hour market are usually enormous (especially the Japanese yen).

Second – Have a good working relationship with your broker for prompt fills and placing or changing orders.

Third – Free yourself from distractions as much as possible during critical trading times such as the opening and closing of the markets. The slightest distraction can cause errors resulting in lost profits and, more importantly, frustration and lack of confidence.

Fourth – Do not be tempted to change your time reference. If you are day trading liquidate your position by the close.

Fifth – The opening price is usually near the high or low of the day approximately 80 percent of the time. Try to trade in the direction of the opening price (i.e., be a buyer when prices are above the opening price, be a seller when prices are below the opening price).

Sixth – Keep your losses small. $300 ($750 in the S&P 500).

Seventh – Don't overtrade! Usually three or four markets can be followed. Know your limitations.

Eighth – respect margin requirements for day trading (25 percent of normal). Don't fall to the temptation of trading more contracts because you are day trading. Risk is the only thing you can control.

Ninth – Take profits when offered. This is not a game of right or wrong. It is about making money.

Tenth – Keep your own counsel Tell no one what you are trading that day. This keeps your mind free to act appropriately.

"...you can learn anything you need to learn to become anyone you want to become, to achieve anything you want to achieve. There are very few limitations and most of them are on the inside, not on the outside."
Brian Tracey— "Maximum Achievement"

The Two Mistakes

There are only two mistakes in trading. The first mistake and the second mistake. Legendary soybean trader Roy Longstreet wrote about this in his classic book, *Viewpoints of a Commodity Trader.* He was known on the street as the king of the soybean market much like Jesse Livermore was known as the king of the bear market.

Longstreet stated that the first mistake teaches. There is no shame in being wrong. Shame results from staying wrong. The second mistake is when traders fail to correct their first mistake. This is when traders face their doom by not admitting that their expectations of market behavior was totally and completely wrong. Truly great traders recognize this and can reverse their position in the market. A difficult thing to do for any trader. Reversing from a long to short (or vice-versa) is this trader's weakest trait. Years of trading have made this my Achilles heel but it is a weakness I have learned to take in stride. My good friend and famous author, Mark Douglas spent considerable time trying to extol the virtues of trading failed patterns. After many months we agreed that my forte was pattern recognition – not failed pattern recognition!

Seeing the first mistake is my strength and not making the killing second mistake has kept me in the hunt for many decades. Recognize when you are wrong. There is great comfort in exiting a losing position and clearing your mind to take the next trade!

"Many years ago, in ancient Greece, a traveler met an old man on the road and asked him how to get to Mount Olympus. The old man who happened to be Socrates, replied by saying, 'If you really want to get to Mount Olympus, just make sure that every step you take is in that direction.'"
An Old Fable from—
"Maximum Achievement," by Brian Tracey

The Watchful Eye

At all times we are under the watchful eye of someone! This is true of trading as it is in all areas of life. This watchful eye acts as a guidance mechanism to let us choose the rightful path to our chosen goal. One of my famous quotes comes from one of my sports heroes – the great catcher of the New York Yankees – Yogi Bera! The great Yogi himself said that when you come to the fork in the road – take it.

Many similar Yogi-isms are known but this is one of my personal favorites. We all have to take the fork in the road (i.e., make decisions) and no where is it more true than in our trading decisions. Luckily, we have a built in computer that watches over us as we select the fork in the road. This mechanism is our inner voice! Your greatest enemy (and friend) is keeping a close eye on you! Listen to what you are feeling and thinking. It's not an immense psychological undertaking. Our minds are the greatest computers in the world, by far! Why do you think God gave us this great decision making tool.

The only way we can utilize this tool is to allow for the quiet time for our minds to process all the information. Quiet time just listening to the voices in our mind. Not all answers will be forthcoming but the solitude will more often than not lead you to the true essence of trading. It is you and *only* you that can determine your success. You are the captain of your fate and the master of your soul. Just listen to yourself – the information is priceless.

Allow for a few minutes before the trading day to listen to your computer. But the key work here is "before" the trading day. Remember, this time does not replace the time for trade preparation. Far from it! It adds to the chemistry to make you a better and more informed trader!

"The ability to set goals and to make plans for their accomplishment is the master skill of success. Developing this skill will do more to ensure your success than anything else you could ever do."
Brian Tracey— "Maximum Achievement"

The Worst Mistakes in Trading

1. – Adding to a losing position.
2. – Trading without a trading plan.
3. – Going for broke!

One of my mentors gave me some sage advice over 30 years ago – "Don't ever go for broke because you just might succeed." Risking everything on one trade is a sure recipe for failure. Even if the trade works you will eventually repeat the lack of money management rules that put you in an "all or nothing" situation. Putting it all on the line for one trade is the by-product of lacking any idea of what trading is all about. It is not about being right or wrong on any one trade. It is a business of making money by using probabilities and risk management!

By the time the trader is in the "go for broke" mode, the process of effective trading has been eliminated. It now becomes a roll of the dice proposition. This is why Las Vegas gambling appeals to some people. There is a built in money management system. When you lose all your money – you get to go home.

Traders get to go home also. If they would take the capital they risked on that last trade and use it for trading education they would have some chance of recovery. I speak from experience on this subject because in 1974 I lost a seven figure account in ten weeks; it became known as the "crash of 1974". In the preceding three years leading up to October of 1974, I had been "on fire" in trading. Trading the long side of a great bull market took zero brains but I didn't see it that way. July of 1974 ushered in a vicious bear market that wiped me out. I proceeded to break every investment rule ever written – some of them many times over. Two years of intense study of my mistakes was followed by many years of success. It was the learning process after the "going for broke" that made speculating so enjoyable.

Spend time examining your mistakes. If you don't you will always confront the cousins, aunts, uncles, brothers and sisters of the mistake family.

"Goals are the fuel in the furnace of achievement. A person without goals is like a ship without a rudder, drifting aimlessly and always in danger of ending up on the rocks. A person with goals is like a ship with a rudder, guided by a captain with a map, a compass, and a destination, sailing straight and true toward a port of his own choosing."

Brian Tracey— "Maximum Achievement"

Think Little

Pete Rose, the great baseball player, once said he would make more money hitting singles than those sluggers who wait for the home runs. Trading is a lot like baseball. You have to score runs but don't rely on the home run. Get your trades to first base, and then second and eventually home by keeping your losses small. Remember Babe Ruth hit over 700 home runs but he also struck out over 5000 times. Joe DiMaggio on the other hand hit only 370 home runs but struck out only 389 times. You have to get on base in order to score.

Keeping your losses small is not an easy task. You should study price action religiously in order to place your orders outside of the normal chaos of the market. Markets are chaotic in nature but within this chaos are the non random patterns that can give the trader using pattern recognition a distinct edge.

Most of your trading profits will be modest gains. Occasionally the markets will reward you with a monster trade (the home run). Enjoy the experience but don't expect it to repeat often.

"What could be more practical than becoming absolutely fearless?"
Guy Finley— "The Lost Secrets of Prayer"

Thinking in Probabilities

It is a given that traders can not win 100 percent of the time, because with reward comes risk, and losses are as much a fact of life as taxes and death. But there are highly valuable lessons to be learned about the trading process that go far beyond dollar signs. How traders put reliable steps in place to ensure that their performance may be enhanced on the road to success is dependent not only on what is done correctly but also on what potentially havoc-wreaking mistakes can be avoided.

The three practical principles that can aid in anticipating and, possibly, avoiding mistakes are *probability, self-discipline* and *responsibility* – simple enough to write, but harder to carry out.

No successful trader would deny that mental preparation is just as necessary as charts and market signals. Trading is all about probabilities and, while every trader encounters a losing streak or draw down of equity, success as a trader is measured by how well losses are handled mentally.

A "sure" sign of potential disaster is holding large losses in open positions while at the same time taking many small profits. This is contrary to the market adage by a wise trader/mentor from Commodity Corporation, Amos Barr Hostetter, who said, *"Take care of your losses and your profits will take care of themselves."* A trader who mentally dupes himself into believing that the small profits will offset the large losses is taking a dangerous ostrich approach.

Most losing streaks are the result of probability distribution. In 100 trades, a system should encounter a losing streak of up to eight trades in a row, and this is the time when the trader begins to question the validity of the system. It also normally is the worst time to stop trading as long as the trader has followed his methodology, because it's been shown that winning streaks generally follow losing streaks.

Examining daily trading logs enables the trader to spot some common trading mistakes such as lack of discipline, sloppiness in trade preparation, impulse trading, impatience, and all of the other cousins and uncles in the "mistake family." One of the big advantages of the pattern recognition method of swing trading is the probability associated with each pattern. Winning is a matter of executing all of the trades as the patterns develop.

Traders must train themselves to think in terms of probability for three very important reasons:

1. No one knows with 100-percent certainty whether the trade will be profitable or not.
2. No one knows how much money will be made or lost on a trade.
3. If the trader does not control the profit outcome and does not know with 100-percent certainty which trades will work,

then the trader should spend 100-percent of his time concentrating on the only element of the trade he *can* control – the risk of the trade.

Key to success is the ability to pinpoint how much one can afford to lose. Winners think "how much can I lose?" while losers think "how much can I win?" This fact is easy to demonstrate. Anyone visiting Las Vegas – has been greeted by brightly colored, flashing slot machines that beckon the full-pocketed tourist with the promise "Win One Million Dollars!" However, no visitor has ever seen a sign that reads, "This machine has taken in three million dollars this year." When the trader truly learns how to think like the "house", the probability of winning is increased.

Thinking about losing requires discipline. By focusing acutely on a trading plan, the probabilities for profits or losses and streaks of each, and risk control, risk-taking becomes more manageable and can give traders the ultimate gift – freedom. In fact, making discipline a daily habit allows traders "to weave a habit of a strand a day of discipline until the cable of discipline is almost unbreakable."

Discipline in trading presents itself in several parts. First, there is preparation. Trading is simple, but it takes time. Many hours of preparation occur *long before* any trade is entered. These steps include:

Mental – Traders must think through what risks are present in the trade, and know in advance how to get out of the trade and at what point. Mental preparation, from my experience, also assumes eliminating or limiting alcohol consumption from Sunday through Thursday of the trading week, because it typically takes up to 24 hours to completely leave the blood system. It's best to have the brain working at an optimal level.

Technical – Methodologies vary by the individual trader. All trading opportunities should be explored. A daily ritual of scanning charts will present many good *opportunities.* This is the time-consuming part of trading. Opportunities, however, do not guarantee profits.

Physical – Traders need to release tension in a positive way. Take time to do some type of exercise like golf, tennis or walking.

Discipline is also necessary on the execution side of trading. Risk control is the most critical element of the trading process. Never forget how a devastating loss can destroy the 'psyche." It damages the trader's soul.

Monitoring a profitable trade in progress also requires discipline – follow the trading plan. Do not be concerned about minuscule fluctuations if your goal is higher. There are two questions that every trader should ask: "Has the market changed since I placed the trade? Can I afford the risk on this trade?" If the answer to both of these questions is "yes" the trader should stay in the trade.

Along with discipline, responsibility plays a significant role in the trading game. Once in the market, the trader alone has responsibility for his or her trading decisions – no one else. Not assuming personal responsibility is like jumping into a fast-moving river without a life jacket in the hopes that there is a lifeguard somewhere on the shore. The trader can keep afloat only if he is responsible for his own destiny. Take joy in the good decisions and learn from the bad ones. Place the orders, close the orders and take the profits. Or, swallow hard, and take the loss if that's the responsible thing to do and your plan points in that direction.

Traders can and do fall into the habit of making excuses about why something went wrong. Again quoting Hostetter, *"Forget your profits, but forget you losses faster."*

Taking responsibility can be improved by including a few steps or reminders in the trading plan. What works for one trader might not work for another. The way to handle this is to place a written statement on the computer. The statement says: Has the pattern in the trade changed from the original pattern? Has the initial price objective been reached?

If the answer to both of these questions is "yes" its time to exit the trade. If the answer is "no" then the trade must continue; trading is a business of dealing with probabilities, *not certainties.* Hostetter held that, "We never know which trades will work; the problem arises when we only 'think' we know."

Probability, discipline and responsibility are traits that every trader should strive to attain. Probability assures that losing streaks will develop just as winning streaks will. What matters are how to recover from those losses. Discipline and responsibility help to prevent devastating losses and aid in recovery. Have the discipline to exit or stay in a trade, and take responsibility for the actions. Again, losses are not 100 percent preventable; however, with the right trading strategies and mental focus, many may be avoided.

"You must do the thing you think you cannot do."
Eleanor Roosevelt (1884-1962)

Thinking vs. Probability

Let's suppose you have just read your evening email and the pick from your favorite newsletter is your favorite stock, Qualcom. The earnings are going to be announced in three weeks. You can hardly contain your excitement because you remember last quarter when it shot up like the Space Shuttle before earnings, there is no way you are going to miss this gravy train.

You pull up a daily chart of Qualcom and see it has been rising on steadily declining volume, except for today when it closed down by 10 points on 3 times the average volume, your MACD has turned down, and your stochastic has turned down and is crossing down through 50. But you know Qualcom will run huge before the earnings announcement. You check option prices and discover you can buy 3 strike prices out for only 18 points in premium. You are going to jump in first thing in the morning. You hardly sleep.

In the above scenario, the trader has taken the available, *neutral* information, and distorted it to suit his belief about the future price action of the stock. Distorting information when making trading decisions can trigger emotions that lead to costly errors.

A few mental triggers that can cause a trader to distort neutral and unbiased information;

- A previous trade with a stock that was successful.
- Following someone else's advice or opinion that is contrary to your own.
- Feeling like you 'need' to make a successful trade.
- Feeling like everyone, except you, is making a lot of money and picking the 'right' trades.
- Not having a thorough understanding of the strategy you are using.
- A previous trade with a stock that was a loser.
- Believing you know what the price will do.
- Not believing the price.

One of the most important skills that a trader can develop is objectivity. Learning to stay in the now moment will help the trader to view the market action as it is unfolding not as they would like it to unfold. This will help the trader to think in probabilities – does this trade have a reasonable edge to profit? If the trade has the criteria the trader can then develop a trading plan including the appropriate amount of risk to take.

Let's take probabilities into consideration and look at how important it is to understanding trading as nothing more than the likelihood of one thing happening over another. If you can learn to identify your strategy with probabilities you will no longer need to base it on anything else and there will never be a trade that you *have* to be in.

There are no traders who trade with the right side of the chart filled in. So what do the good traders know or do that you don't? Why does it seem so effortless? I'll sidetrack here to illustrate this point.

Several years ago, I was bitten by the 'ski-bug' I was bound and determined to ski like the smooth and effortless skiers I would watch in awe of as I rode up the chair lift.

It was my good fortune to have signed up for lessons with Brian, who I can only describe as a "ski god".

During our first lesson, we were going down a very gentle slope; Brian asked me what my goals were for that year. At the very moment he asked and I started to answer, my ski tips crossed which in effect tripped me and sent me into a head over heels fall on my back. As I was sliding down the hill, in a sort of Yoga twisted position, Brian was gracefully following me down the hill. I told him, as I was sliding down the hill, that I seemed to have a problem with my ski tips crossing and I didn't know why but I would like to work on it. As I came to a stop next to a tree Brian just said, "I think we can fix that."

The next year, I was riding up the chair lift with Brian; I asked him how his skiing became so fluid and consistent. This man glides down mogul runs and is never out of breath. He is solid and graceful on his skis. He skis all terrain the same, ice, moguls, crud, powder, mixed, it doesn't matter. His reply? "Once I took out of my skiing what didn't work and replaced it with what did work I realized there are no bad snow days, just bad skiers."

Skiing is very technical, much like a technical approach to trading. You learn in steps, or progressions. If you fall you can analyze the cause and then add or remove something to change the outcome the next time. Sometimes on days when I see a lot of skiers turning in their tickets because "you can't ski on that stuff" I smile to myself and head for the lift. There are no bad snow days!

Now back to trading…

You want to identify at what point you will enter a trade that will give you an edge. At what point will there be a higher probability of one thing happening over another? **Not a guarantee**, but a higher than 50% chance of that outcome. There are some very good traders that have a strategy that is below 50% and still make consistent profits. By taking the time to study a strategy so that you know it and have a high confidence level in it, you will greatly increase your trading successes.

One of your goals should be to fine-tune your trading skills so that you are able to take in and look at available information objectively. This takes time, patience and practice. You will make mistakes and sometimes overlook the most obvious things. When this happens, go easy on yourself and correct what needs to be corrected the best you can. If you need to sell, then sell. If you missed an entry point, don't chase it. You can wait for another entry or find another trade. Start to take note of when you feel you have 'distorted' the information. If you keep track you will be able to spot it sooner and take the appropriate actions.

When you distort the information, you are trying to get the price to conform to your expectations, rather than evaluating what the most likely direction of price is in "X" time period? If you can start to be objective you can then view the charts that come along in categories; **1**. Those that are ready to buy.

2. Those that are ready to sell. **3**. Those that do not give enough information to determine a reasonable probability. In a nutshell, buy, hold or sell.

Once this process starts, you will no longer find blame with anybody or thing but yourself. Except, when you take a loss you will no longer blame yourself, but congratulate yourself for doing what is necessary to become a successful and consistent trader. You will then be on the right path. You will start to see that your 'thinking' can actually interfere with your process. I don't mean that you should take thinking out of trading, I mean when you 'think' you know what prices will do you start a mental process that can lock you into that thought and everything you take in will be distorted to fit that opinion.

If you study charts, you'll begin to realize that every chart will offer an opportunity to profit. Prices do not stay in one place. Keep this in mind when you find yourself focusing on one trade that isn't going well. I call this tunnel vision. You get so wound up about one trade that you don't see a dozen other good trades going by.

If you use a newsletter service to help pick your trades it is a good idea to never take any 'picks' on blind faith. In other words, you don't quite have a strategy so you attempt to use theirs. Remember that they know the method they use like the back of their hand. They are not trading based on one trade. They trade based on many trades and know that some work, some don't. If you pick just one trade out of the many available, your odds of success decrease dramatically. You need to do a series of trades using the same strategy to really evaluate the success. Many strategies are suited for some types of markets and perform well under certain conditions. You need to know what those are. If you happen to start trading a strategy during market conditions that are not likely to give good results for a period but would normally outperform in other types of market conditions, you need to be aware of this. It would be very easy to pass by a very good trading system because of this.

A series of trades, say 100, based on one strategy may produce some great winners, some good winners, some scratched trades and some losers, not necessarily in that order. Out of those trades, ***nobody knows which ones will be which!*** Now, hopefully you are starting to see that we are talking about probabilities. Not hoping or wishing. You should be able to answer if the system you use has a high probability of one thing happening over another. Should I be in this trade or out? If I am in the trade then ***why*** am I in the trade. There should only be one answer- the probabilities of success are on your side.

This is very important to understand so that you know when your system is likely to perform well and when you might want to sit it out.

Losses are inevitable in trading. Go back to the 100-trade scenario; do you or anybody know which of those trades will be the great winners, the losers, the breakevens or the average gainer? If you know that, you don't need a system.

Whatever style of trading you choose you must develop a high confidence level in it to be able to assess the probabilities and execute the trades properly. If you do this you will start to eliminate many of the mental problems and stresses that come with trading.

Remember, we all started on the Bunny hill. But with time, hard work, good teachers and mentors you *can* make it to the tougher slopes!

"And the trouble is, if you don't risk anything, you risk even more."
Erica Jong—American Writer

Time is on Your Side

Many people are drawn to trading for many different reasons. Out of the vast numbers a large percentage seem to want to speed up the learning curve sacrificing learning valuable pieces of information on the way. Trading is a skill that is developed and fine tuned over a lifetime. It would be helpful to the novice trader to resolve themselves that the process can be lengthy and that no one can put a specific time on how long it will take.

Mastery of anything requires time, perseverance and a strong desire to know the subject inside and out. As with anything there are two sides to learning trading; the approach or method that will be used and second; the correct mindset to apply that approach or method. There are hundreds of small steps involved in learning to trade well that add up to a larger picture.

Here is a thought that I hope will encourage a novice trader to enjoy the process and realize that *all* the steps are necessary, even the painful ones, and resign themselves to however long their personal journey takes them: Trading is a journey, if you miss one step or several steps in the process one of them just might be the key for you that would put it all together. Think of it in these terms, if you were putting together a jigsaw puzzle and decided to randomly remove several pieces of the puzzle that puzzle would never be complete without those pieces. Each piece, no matter how small, must be in place in order for the larger picture to be viewed in full.

"Life is what happens to you when you're making other plans."
Betty Talmadge—American meat broker

TRADE PREPARATION

Trading is a lot like golf. It takes certain skills which require a lot of practice. A mind set is necessary to play out the scenarios on the course. And most important, it is necessary to know when you reach the 18th green or decide to take a double bogey to reduce the damage. Everyone would like to play golf with Tiger Woods – but who among us is willing to hit the 20,000 golf balls to play at Tiger Wood's level!

Pattern recognition trading is a probability based system. Each pattern has its own payoff and risk parameter. Pattern recognition falls into one of the categories of technical analysis. Technical analysis has been the wicked step sister of market information – almost like a witch's brew. But things are changing radically thanks to a boost from our friends in academia, this time it was the prestigious group from the Massachusetts Institute of Technology (MIT). Colleagues of Dr. Andrew Lo ran sophisticated statistical studies to prove once and for all that chart patterns have no use in the investment community. What they discovered was astounding to everyone except those of us who have been profitably trading chart patterns for years.

Dr. Lo's group found amazing correlations in price patterns and these patterns did repeat with regularity and could be mathematically quantified. The complete article was published in Business Week. [1]

Each day I track the 40 most active and volatile stocks! (20 NYSE and 20 NASDAQ). My favorites are JPM, AXP, INTC, MSFT, CSCO, GE, etc.

The SP 500 futures, 10 year note and t-bond/dollar/yen charts are also followed. Within these 40 or so charts, several patterns will be tradable set-ups for the next few days or possibly a day trading opportunity. The SP 500 is the only vehicle I trade everyday – it provides a speculators dream – volatility, liquidity, low commission and most importantly, good execution.

At the end of each days trading, I review the 40 plus charts. First I check for the daily patterns, next I scale down to the 30-min patterns. Finally, as a trade is setting up I go to the 4 minute charts for entry. The patterns on all of the charts are recognizable. Four-minute charts allow me to estimate sales volume and the bid and ask spreads. I use four-minute charts because the earth rotates one degree every four minutes making it a natural cycle.

Next step is to wait for the pattern to complete and enter the market, i.e. jump in the river, knowing with 100% certainty that you can never know how much you can make, (if anything). So always have your life raft with you (stop protection), if you want to get out of the river. Drowning is not an acceptable outcome!

1 This alchemy may yield real gold. *Business Week*. April 17, 2000, p.170.

"You can't be brave if you've only had wonderful things happen to you."
Mary Tyler Moore—American Actress

Trader in Crises

Life isn't as smooth as we would like it to be. As traders we must be aware of those times when family and health issues are placed on the front burner of life and trading must take a back seat.

During my years at Commodity Corporation it became clear that the two most dangerous events in a trader's personal life are divorce and death. Each has many issues connected deep into our psyche. A trader working under one of these events must be very cognizant of every thing they do. If both death and divorce are present, trading should cease and professional help sought. Personally, I have never seen a positive trading experience in any of my friends or trading buddies that experienced either of the big "D's"! Keep in mind that this is over a 40-year period and involves a large sample size as well.

There is an old Chinese proverb that aptly describes this situation, *"A smart man learns from his mistakes, the wise man learns from the mistakes of others."* Since all of us will be exposed to these events at some point in our trading life, it would behoove us to recognize the danger signs when they are present:

1. Lack of interest in trading.
2. Failure to prepare and execute properly.
3. Use of alcohol and antidepressants.
4. Disregarding the trading plan.
5. Over trading.
6. Trading over margin limits.
7. Lack of interest in personal health.

These are just some of the signs that *scream* out to us "I need help!" They can be overcome through therapy and time. Trading is fun and profitable – don't let a crisis ruin it all.

"...the greater part of our happiness or misery depends on our dispositions and not on our circumstances."
Martha Washington (1731-1802)

Trading as a Profession

When my daughters were small they would always ask me what I did for a living. It is difficult enough to explain it to an adult – explaining it to a 6-year-old is impossible. I am a speculator. Speculator is a derivative of the Latin "speculare", which means to "see"! I try to see opportunity. It's ironic that the Chinese letter for opportunity and risk are the same. The context of the sentence determines its meaning.

Speculation (i.e. trading) is a noble profession because it provides three elements necessary for capitalization. First – transfer of risk from one party to another. Second – it provides liquidity for the movement of capital. Third – it provides a profit motive for the individual in the transaction.

The financial press loves to embellish the similarities of speculating and gambling. Nothing could be further from the truth. Gambling creates a risk when none existed before, such as the roll of the dice, spin of the wheel and the outcome of a football game. Trading has a transfer of risk from one party to another. This allows one of the parties (or both) to hedge or transfer the risk. This transaction is similar to an insurance policy. When an insured event occurs, the insuring party pays off the policy.

Tuition costs for the speculator's profession can be prohibitive. Studies have shown that 90% of all first time traders lose. Those that remain and can survive the next three years will be ready to start consistent profitable trading. This makes it equivalent in cost and time to a college education.

As the time arrives when you are a successful trader, you can look in the mirror and feel proud. It's the only adulation you will get because there are no commencement exercises. There are no final tests or certification. Your daily position statement will be the source of your strength.

If you are really one of the lucky ones, a neophyte trader asking for help will approach you. This wake-up call is your chance to help a fellow human being start a career that Confucius described: *"Find a job you love and you will always be on a vacation."*

"If you have made mistakes...there is always another chance for you...you may have a fresh start any moment you choose, for this thing we call "failure" is not the falling down, but the staying down."

Mary Pickford (1893-1979) American actress

Trading Fatigue

Trading on a full time basis as a professional requires a great deal of energy. Like all professions there will be times when you will be asked to perform your daily tasks at less than peak performance levels.

Psychological and physiological effects such as family crisis and personal health issues can bring on fatigue. Let's just look at the area of trading fatigue. Probably the most obvious is overtrading. If you are looking at one-minute charts you are found guilty without trial. I do not know one successful trader that can maintain this energy level. Staring into that silly monitor will make you cuckoo!

Your energy level must be kept near peak levels, both physically and mentally. Good diet, exercise and meditation go a long way to increasing your profit and loss statement in a positive way.

Fatigue contributes to damaging a trader's soul. That love for the business and looking forward to the next trading opportunity diminishes with fatigue. Professional athletes find their work ethics and stick to them.

Develop your own daily routines and make them a habit. Remember that a habit is like a tiny strand of steel that you weave each day until it becomes an unbreakable cable!

"Mistakes are part of the dues one pays for a full life."
Sophia Loren—Italian actress

Trading Ghosts

Trading is a journey not a destination but the baggage we bring to the table can make the journey both long and hard. And all traders have them! That is the good news. The bad news is your failure to correct the baggage that prevents consistently profitable trading will continue to plague your bottom line.

Traders are human and we all have an 'Achilles heel". Those elusive ghosts that seem to know when our "psyche" is at its most vulnerable point often come out to haunt us. Knowledge of the weakness is the first step to correct the problem.

"If you know your enemy your are strong, but if you know yourself you are omnipotent" – Sun Tsu from 'Art of War' (circa 600 b.c.)

Several things can be done to help ward off your trading ghosts – read books on the psychology of trading. Two of my favorites are the *Disciplined Trader* and *Trading in the Zone* by Mark Douglas. His *Trading in the Zone* book I read religiously each day. After reading it thoroughly the first time I decided to develop a habit to read 5 pages each day (7 days a week). A habit is like a steel cable, you weave a strand a day until it becomes almost unbreakable. At the end of the year I have been through it four times. Mark's work seems to be pointing to me (and all traders) and his description of how you must learn to think in probabilities.

Also of value are self help books and audio tapes from Anthony Robbins. Robbins uses Neuro Linguistic training that links the body's responses to new transmitters. I did my first "walk on fire" at a function of Anthony Robbins. There are many other self help books each of which has something useful. Trading is a journey and books make the trip more enjoyable and educational!

"It is hard to fight an enemy who has outposts in your head."
Sally Kempton—American writer

Trading in Fear

Fear is the greatest obstacle to successful trading. It is fear that is the culprit! Fear causes us to freeze, delay, act too quickly and at its worst makes us totally irrational in our trading behavior. The irony when dealing with fear is that most of our fears are never realized. The acronym for fear is:

False **E**vidence **A**ppearing **R**eal

All of us can remember as children the shadows of monsters in our room and in the trees as we walked at night. It is the same emotion that we face everyday when trading. But you must be able to recognize your fear and face it head on!

Death should have no fear associated with it. The fear should be not living a full life because of fear. *"All men die – some men never live,"* from a Scottish proverb. Try to live each day to its fullest because you never know when the final bell is going to toll!

The battle against overcoming fear will most likely be a life long process. But with some effort and daily positive affirmations, fear can be overcome. Keep in mind one fact that will never change, and this will stay with us as long as we live, we will all die eventually so live well and enjoy the process.

"...You may be disappointed if you fail, but you are doomed if you don't try."
Beverly Sills—American opera singer

Trading is a Journey – Not a Destination!

As soon as you can accept that trading is a business of accepting losses, the sooner consistent success will come and stay! Losses are like breathing; you have to have them in order to stay alive. It is the neophyte trader that won't take his loss and it is that trade that buries them. The loss itself is devastating but the damage that it does to the soul (psyche) remains for a long time, sometimes forever.

There are only three things that can happen when you put on a trade:

1. You win
2. You lose
3. You break even

Can it be any easier? Why emotionalize over a trading situation that is out of your control. The worse thing that you can do is focus on all the upticks and downticks while staring at your monitor.

What can a trader do to take the emotion out of the equation? First, place orders before the market opens and leave. Stops and contingency orders will be placed at that time. Remember that no one can tell you what amount of money you will make on the trade. The only thing you can control is the amount at risk.

Men and women are not judged by how they handle success – they are measured by how they pick themselves up after a failure. A small child doesn't stop trying to walk after the first fall.

Opinions on what the market is going to do can also effect trading. *"Lose your opinion instead of your money"* – Paul Tudor Jones. Great advice from a great trader!

Enjoy the trading process and it can enrich your life in many ways. In the end we all die anyway!

"Light tomorrow with today!"
Elizabeth Barret Browning—
English Poet (1806-1861)

Trading Out of Control

At some time or another in a trader's life he or she reaches a point where they go on tilt. Normally it occurs after a prolonged period of trading without a break! But trading fatigue is not the only culprit. Market opinions are the single largest source of our frustrations in the market. It is a blow to our analysis and pride when the market fails to respond to our expectations. Experienced traders have learned to brush off the opinion and trade what they see and not what they believe. *"Lose your opinion instead of your money"* – Paul Tudor Jones.

There are tell- tale signs of trading out of control. One of the most dangerous is trading without stop loss orders. Afraid of missing the big one, the trader wishfully believes the market will turn and vindicate his esteem. Overtrading is another symptom as well as trading without a trading plan. The whole purpose of a trading plan is to prevent this from happening. The rules in your trading plan can be flexible within normal risk limits based on your trading equity.

Sometimes the trader does not recognize that a break from trading is needed until the damage has been done. Consider a checklist that monitors your own trading and would alert you to some of these warning signs. Try and take breaks from trading that completely remove you mentally and physically from trading. A daily regiment of regular sleep patterns, eating and physical exercise are very important for trading performance.

Know what your own limitations are and then book a vacation!

"We don't see things as they are,
we see them as we are."
Anais Nin—American writer (1903-1977)

Trading with a Plan!

You would not send your son or daughter off to college without them having a curriculum for study. But most speculators (investors) give the application of sound trading or investing strategies very little thought. They either listen to their broker, neighbor, colleagues or friends for tips on the market. Or they listen to one of the financial channels or trade publications such as Wall Street Journal, Barrons or Investors Business Daily, totally unaware that the news follows the prices. By the time the good news hits the airwaves prices have already been moving in that direction (bullish or bearish).

A sound trading plan can take you out of the news loop. There are three elements in a trading plan;

First – The reason for the trade. This can be technically based or fundamentally based or a combination of both. What I use with considerable success has been the pattern recognition technique of swing trading.

Second – The trading plan should have specific entry and exit points. This will define the risk in the trade. Always remember that you never know which trades will work or the profit available in any trade! Given these two known tenets the only thing a trader can control is the amount of risk in the trade.

Third – The emotional foundation to follow steps one and two. The plan is not meant to be rigid but it can not be changed on a whim.

Amos Barr Hostetter, founder of Commodity Corporation, had two rules for exiting a position;

1. Has the position reached the designated price target?
2. Has anything occurred that causes the original position to be suspect?

If you can answer yes to either of these questions the position should be liquidated.

These are some guidelines that can help you develop your own trading plan and rules.

"Adventure is something you seek for pleasure, or even for profit, like a gold rush or invading a country;...but experience is what really happens to you in the long run; the truth that finally overtakes you."

Katherine Anne Porter—American writer (1903-1977)

Trading without Capital

Several things are present in the equation to be a successful trader! The Trading Plan – The Mental Attitude – The Trading Capital.

In my opinion, each part has a different weighting. Mental Attitude is 70% - Trading Plan 20% (although your Mental Attitude can affect your Trading Plan 100 %!) and the least important is the trading capital. There is an old joke (somewhat sick) in our business and it goes something like this; "The best way to make a small fortune in trading is to start with a large fortune." No Universities teach comprehensive classes on learning to speculate. There are some classes to be sure but nothing substantial. Thirty years ago I taught an evening graduate class in investments and little has been added since that time.

Traders are left in the wind to set their own sails. Entering into the investment forum is easy. You have to have some money and be able to sign your name on the account forms.

Your first clue is the account forms! Warnings of high risk are everywhere on these forms. There is a reason for this. The brokerage firms want to prevent litigation if they go array (as they often do). Multiple warnings are present in the forms for commodities and options. But speculators flock to the open doors of the first bastion of capitalism ill equipped to face some of the high seasoned traders of the world.

Faced with this challenge, thousands still enter the game. Beginning traders fail at the rate of 80% or higher. However, those that stick with it can usually expect positive results between one and five years. Amazingly similar to the length of a college education.

Marty Schwartz, author of *The Pit Bull*, revealed that it was 10 years before he was able to become consistently profitable. There is hope for all traders. Winston Churchill's most famous speech was at the depths of depression in World War II. Walking on stage, the great statesman uttered these famous words; *"Never give up! Never, Never, Never!"* He then quietly left the stage.

Read books and articles on the subjects you will need, Technical, Fundamental and Psychological. Find a methodology that suits your own "Psyche." Working with a seasoned veteran trader (a mentor) is the quickest way to learn. *"The smart man learns from his mistakes – the wise man learns from the mistakes of others."*

"The only thing that makes life possible is permanent, intolerable uncertainty; not knowing what comes next."
Ursula K Leguin—American writer

Trouble

Trouble can wear many disguises! It will not always be cloaked in a sinister garb with an eerie foreboding of bad things to come. Sometimes trouble will be right behind one of the traders biggest and most successful trading campaigns.

Because trouble comes without warning in most instances it is necessary for the trader to always be vigilant of it lurking around. It is one of the reasons that trading is a mental game. Acknowledging that you are always challenged mentally can be your armor against the appearance of trouble.

There are several early warning signs of trouble. One sign can be over-trading. A second sign can be wider than normal swings in the trader's equity. Still another sign, which is the most dangerous, is the failure to follow the trader's plan!

There are two easy exercises that should help spot signs of trouble. They are so important that they should be included as part of the daily trading ritual.

First – keep a daily trading diary. Just a few short notes on what you did well and what could have been improved. It doesn't need to be an essay. When things go wrong this will help spot inconsistencies in various parts of the trading plan.

Second – read four or five pages of Mark Douglas' book, *Trading in the Zone* before each trading day. This acts as stretching exercises for the mind of the trader and puts the emphasis on the mental aspects of trading. At the end of one year you will have read the book several times!

The important thing to remember is that you find a daily ritual to face trouble when it arises. Never, never hide from trouble – it will just get worse.

"The key to overcoming fear of failure is breaking one's attachment to results. Whenever we convince ourselves that results are all that count, we fall into anxiety that paradoxically limits our ability to achieve results..."
R. E. McMaster, Jr.—
"Trader's Notebook 1"

TRUTH

"Truth kills those that run from it" – Persian Proverb

Traders must be able to face the truth. Great traders have learned these lessons early in their careers. Roy Longstreet in his classic book *Viewpoints of a Commodity Trader* stated that *"the first mistake teaches – the second mistake kills!"*

Facing the truth in trading is necessary to prevent the consequences. Truth is necessary at all levels of trading. It is just as important to the novice as it is to the seasoned veteran. The main difference lies in the ability to face the truth.

Truth seems so simple! But the psyche can do amazing tricks through rationalization. Some of these tricks seem to have no other purpose than to prevent you from seeing the reality of the truth.

The Bible states – *"The truth shall set you free."* Every religion has a saying echoing the same theme. Overcoming not facing the truth can be accomplished by writing down the pros and cons of telling the truth. Once it is committed to paper the decision should become self-evident. My grandmother used to tell me *"if you tell the truth at 10 am you won't have to remember at 2 pm."* This is really sage advice that works well in the trading arena.

"It is amazing how much we can learn out of every situation if we first assume that every problem is our own fault. If a problem is our fault, we can move to solve it."
R. E. McMaster—
"Trader's Notebook 1"

Two Emotions

There are two emotions that appear in the trading environment with a great deal of regularity. Fear and anger are the culprits of many trading mistakes. Between the two evils one is better to have than the other. Anger is better than fear because anger and fear cannot be present at the same time. Anger is our way of fighting back fear. Fear is the most dangerous because it exits in our minds. Most fears never materialize. As Anthony Robbins quotes *"Fear is false evidence appearing real."*

Once the anger subsides a chance exists for reason to enter the equation. Reason is the one thing the trader must possess to make the logical decisions necessary for trading successfully.

Professional traders have developed the necessary skills to combat both anger and fear. However, these skills are acquired. A sound trading plan based on probability theory and money management will overcome both emotions of anger and fear.

There is a caveat that must be mentioned here; outside influences can bring out anger and fear. A perfect example was the September 11th attack on the World Trade Center. Fortunately, the markets closed for four days for only the second time in history. Personally, it was the most emotional trading period of my 40 years as a trader.

Most often the anger comes from personal involvement with a loved one such as a spouse or child, or from a business associate. Both can have negative consequences on trading results and it would be wise for a trader to consider halting their trading activities until these emotions are under control.

"It is a truth very certain that when it is not in our power to determine what is true we ought to follow what is most probable."
Descartes, "Discourse on Method," 1637

What Do You Do When You Are Losing?

Every trader encounters a losing streak or draw down of equity. Trading is all about probabilities. There will be winning streaks as well as losing streaks. Success in a trader is measured in how well he handles his losses because if all of his capital is depleted, he is no longer in the business.

A "sure" sign of potential disaster is the trader who holds large losses in open positions while at the same time takes many small profits. This is exactly against the market adage *"Take care of your losses and your profits will take care of themselves."* – A.B Hostetter

Most losing streaks are the result of probability distribution. In 100 trades your system should encounter a losing streak of up to eight trades in a row. This is the time when the trader begins to questions the validity of a system. It is also the worst time to stop trading as long as the trader has followed his methodology because losing streaks are followed by winning streaks.

Examining their daily trading log will enable the trader to spot some common trading mistakes such as lack of discipline, sloppiness in trade preparation, over trading (impulse trading), impatience and all of the other cousins and uncles of the mistake family. One of the big advantages of the pattern recognition method of swing trading is the probabilities associated with each pattern. Winning is simply a matter of executing all of the trades as the patterns develop. Remember that you must train yourself to think in terms of probability for three very important reasons:

1. No one knows with 100% certainty whether the trade will win or lose.
2. No one knows how much money will be made on the trade.
3. What is left is the only variable the trader can control and that is the amount of risk capital afforded to each trade.

Learn to think about how much you can lose - Winners think how much can I lose, Losers think how much can I win! This fact is easy to demonstrate. The next time you visit Las Vegas take a look at the beautiful flashing slot machines that beckon the gambler with promises of "Win 1 Million Dollars"! Casinos would never put a sign up that said, "This machine has taken in 3 million dollars this year." When the trader learns how to think like the "house", then he has increased his probability of winning.

"Our inner thoughts, beliefs, self-perceptions, and emotions can give us a lift for a positive outcome, or hold us back in complete inertia."
Dr. Phil McGraw—
"Ultimate Weight Solution"

When in Doubt

There is a large oil painting behind my trading desk depicting the patterns I use and the most important market tenets I've found that work for me. It was painted by one of my customers back in the old days at Drexel Burnham Lambert.

Tenet number 2 is – **When in doubt – get out and stay out**. Traders need an edge and doubt is not an edge, it's a hatchet! You must believe in your trading methodology. If not you are lost in an ocean infected with trading-eating sharks. You are trading against some of the finest minds in the world but you are also trading against your strongest enemy – yourself.

Trading and sports have much in common. They leave the winners with the exhilaration of winning and the losers with the agony of defeat.

Doubt is destructive! It leaves many unanswered questions. There can be no doubt when putting on a trade. Who cares whether it wins or loses! It's only a probability anyway! Move on to the next trade – hopefully doubt free.

"You must do the thing you think you cannot do."
Eleanor Roosevelt (1884-1962)

Winning Streaks vs. Losing Streaks

All traders who last long enough will go through periods of winning and losing streaks. Mathematicians refer to the process as the theory or run known to gamblers as a "streak." Games of chance such as roulette, craps and blackjack are predicated that the house has an edge over the player. Trading has a distinct advantage because the trader has the ability to be the house. A mathematical edge is all that is needed by the trader to increase his probability of success. Sound money management principles will keep the trader in the game until the mathematical advantage begins to work. What happens in real time trading is that after a series of losing trades the trader will begin to question the system or his ability to execute the system properly.

Two things are necessary to get through the bad losing times! Belief in your system is very important but it ranks second to the sound money management system. Mediocre trading systems can have positive results with the use of a good money management system. The rule of thumb is to reduce your risk on any trade to 2% of working capital. This should prevent a meltdown but remember trading is about probability not certainty!

"...since thoughts are behaviors, you must be alert to what payoffs, or rewards, you are getting from the things you tell yourself. At some level your self-talk is working for you."
Dr. Phil McGraw—
"Ultimate Weight Solution"

Wish List

Early on in my trading career I used to try and make money on a trade to pay for some toy, a vacation, a piece of jewelry, etc. I was laboring under the false assumption that the market would issue me a paycheck for my toils as a trader. Nothing could be further from reality! The market never pays you anything – you pay yourself and the price sometimes is more than your wildest dreams!

Wishing is a great escape but don't factor it into your trading. Just the facts – only the facts! The risk, the potential reward and the probability of an expected positive outcome on the trade. Focus your energies on learning to do the right thing when implementing a trade. Mark Douglas spent hours getting this point across to me. It takes only so many whacks to the head for the importance to get through to me.

Mark illustrated the importance of doing the right thing by using the following illustration. Place the thing you want to wish for right in front of your face. Gaze at it as though it were already there. Now the important step! Take the trade strategy (entry, exit, stop protection, profit objective and move it in front of the wish list. The wish list is now in the background. And that is where is should stay! Concentrate on doing the right thing and the money will come easily! Why, because your focus must be on the proper execution and not what the outcome might be! Remember we never know if the trade will work and we never know what the profit will be! All that is left is the only factor that is under our control – the control of risk on the trade – *"Take care of your losses and your profits will take care of themselves!"* Amos Barr Hostetter.

"Only by optimistically accepting our potential losses can we face the risk and move on to effective action."
Richard D. McCall—
"The Way of the Warrior Trader"

You against the World

Trading can be a lonely business! It is you against the world. Think of your computer monitor for a moment. It acts more like a mirror than a monitor. The face in the monitor cannot hide from its fears, its flaws, and its strength. There is only one fact that matters – *"to thine ownself be true."*

As traders, we have more opinions on where the market is going than ever before. We have twenty-four hour financial television, countless magazines, and daily as well as weekly financial newspapers. Add the thousands of market newsletters and you can sense the information overload. It comes down to just you at the end of the phone line ready to place an order. You are by yourself! You reap the rewards or pay the price. This fact alone is evidence enough to keep your own counsel.

There is one simple thing at the trader's disposal that can keep him on the right path! Do the "**right**" thing! This requires thinking about what you are doing. Don't focus on the money involved. Focus on the longer picture of your mental health.

Bad trading mistakes do far more damage to the trader's soul than they ever do to the financial ledger.

By focusing on doing the right thing, trading can be a profound learning experience as well as profitable.

"In all of your adversities lie the seeds of equivalent advantages. In every defeat there is a lesson showing you how to win the next time."
Unknown

YOUR EPITAPH

Few of us would ever think of writing our own epitaph in preparation for the inevitable journey into the after life. Fear of facing our own mortality is the main reason. Whether it is important or not to have it written is a matter for conjecture anyway.

There is one particular and famous epitaph on a shallow rock grave in the city of Tombstone, Arizona. Lester Moore was shot in 1882 during the violent uprising of crime popularized by novels and movies featuring the life and times of Wyatt Earp. Wyatt Earp and his three brothers were acting sheriffs in Tombstone. Lester Moore was one of the 20 or so citizens of Tombstone. The city was a Silver mining town and larger than Los Angeles, Ca. In the late 1800's. But what the heck does any of this have to do with trading?

On one of my tourist visits to Tombstone, I looked forward to visiting "Boot Hell" where all the old cowboys are buried. Approaching the grave of Lester Moore stopped me dead in my tracks (pardon the pun). The gravestone read:

"Here Lies Lester Moore

Shot 6 times with a 44

No Les – More

October 1882"

At first, it seems almost funny, but after realizing that you are in a National Jewish Cemetery it takes on a more somber experience.

This experience reminded me how short life can be. And it can be ended abruptly. The key is in getting as much enjoyment as possible in the time allotted. Since our allotment is unknown then the obvious solution is to live each day as though it was the last or one of the last. Lester Moore certainly didn't expect to be shot six times.

You don't have to throw caution to the wind! Just enjoy yourself and your family and friends. That's what really counts in life.

"I think that wherever your journey takes you, there are new gods waiting there, with divine patience—and laughter."

—Susan M. Watkins—American writer

Autobiography in Five Short Chapter
by Portia Nelson

Chapter I

I walk down the street.
There is a deep hole in the sidewalk.
I fall in.
I am lost...I am hopeless.
It isn't my fault.
It takes forever to find a way out.

Chapter II

I walk down the same street.
There is a deep hole in the sidewalk.
I **pretend** I don't see it.
I fall in again.
I can't believe I am in this same place.
But it isn't my fault.
It still takes a long time to get out.

Chapter III

I walk down the same street.
There is a deep hole in the sidewalk.
I **see** it there.
I still fall in...it's a habit...but,
my eyes are open.
I know where I am.
It is **my** fault.
I get out immediately.

Chapter IV

I walk down the same street.
There is a deep hole in the sidewalk.
I walk around it.

Chapter V

I walk down another street.

Larry Pesavento

Larry is a trading mentor and thirty-year veteran of the capital markets. In his career he has been a member of the Chicago Mercantile Exchange, supervised Drexel Burnham Lambert's commodity department in Los Angeles, traded on and off the floor and trained over 300 traders. He is currently a contract trader for a large hedge fund.

Larry seeks to distill and share his thirty years of market experience. His contribution is to teach others the "art and science' of trading, and he periodically gives seminars on his pattern recognition style of trading. His website **www.tradingtutor.com** is a teaching tool for those interested in his pattern recognition method.

You can reach Larry via e-mail at: **larry@tradingtutor.com**

Leslie Jouflas

Prior to starting a full time trading career in 2000, Leslie worked for an airline based on the west coast for 17 years. Leslie has been trading her own account since 1996 and has also begun trading private managed money as well as for a private hedge fund. She also enjoys teaching and encouraging new students to the field of trading. Leslie met Larry Pesavento several years ago at a 5 day workshop that he was teaching. She studied his methodology of pattern recognition with Fibonacci ratios and has adapted that into her trading. She primarily trades futures with a focus on the S&P 500. Leslie can be reached at frredrica@msn.com

Published by: Traders Press, Inc.®

7 Secrets Every Commodity Trader Needs to Know (Mound)
A Complete Guide to Trading Profits (Paris)
A Professional Look at S&P Day Trading (Trivette)
A Treasury of Wall Street Wisdom (Editors: Schultz & Coslow)
Ask Mr. EasyLanguage (Tennis)
Beginner's Guide to Computer Assisted Trading (Alexander)
Channels and Cycles: A Tribute to J.M. Hurst (Millard)
Chart Reading for Professional Traders (Jenkins)
Commodity Spreads: Analysis, Selection and Trading Techniques (Smith)
Comparison of Twelve Technical Trading Systems (Lukac, Brorsen, & Irwin)
Complete Stock Market Trading and Forecasting Course (Jenkins)
Cyclic Analysis (J.M. Hurst)
Dynamic Trading (Miner)
Exceptional Trading: The Mind Game (Roosevelt)
Fibonacci Ratios with Pattern Recognition (Pesavento)
Futures Spread Trading: The Complete Guide (Smith)
Geometry of Markets (Gilmore)
Geometry of Stock Market Profits (Jenkins)
Harmonic Vibrations (Pesavento)
How to Trade in Stocks (Livermore & Smitten)
Hurst Cycles Course (J.M. Hurst)
Investing by the Stars (Weingarten)
Investor Skills Training: Managing Emotions and Risk in the Market (Ronin)
It's Your Option (Zelkin)
Magic of Moving Averages (Lowry)
Market Rap: The Odyssey of a Still-Struggling Commodity Trader (Collins)
Overcoming 7 Deadly Sins of Trading (Roosevelt)
Planetary Harmonics of Speculative Markets (Pesavento)
Point & Figure Charting (Aby)
Point & Figure Charting: Commodity and Stock Trading Techniques (Zieg)
Private Thoughts From a Trader's Diary (Pesavento & MacKay)
Profitable Patterns for Stock Trading (Pesavento)
RoadMap to the Markets (Busby)
RSI: The Complete Guide (Hayden)
Short-Term Trading with Price Patterns (Harris)
Single Stock Futures: The Complete Guide (Greenberg)
Stock Patterns for Day Trading (2 volumes) (Rudd)
Stock Trading Techniques Based on Price Patterns (Harris)
Technically Speaking (Wilkinson)
Technical Trading Systems for Commodities and Stocks (Patel)
The Amazing Life of Jesse Livermore: World's Greatest Stock Trader (Smitten)
The Handbook of Global Securities Operations (O'Connell & Steiniger)
The Opening Price Principle: The Best Kept Secret on Wall Street (Pesavento & MacKay)
The Professional Commodity Trader (Kroll)
The Taylor Trading Technique (Taylor)
*The Trading Rule That Can Make You Rich** (Dobson)
Top Traders Under Fire (Collins)
Trading Secrets of the Inner Circle (Goodwin)
Trading S&P Futures and Options (Lloyd)
Twelve Habitudes of Highly Successful Traders (Roosevelt)
Understanding Bollinger Bands (Dobson)
Understanding Eminis: Trading to Win (Williams)
Understanding Fibonacci Numbers (Dobson)
Viewpoints of a Commodity Trader (Longstreet)
Winning Edge 4 (Toghraie)
Winning Market Systems (Appel)